THE BOOK THAT CHANGED MY LIFE

7 Things Wealthy Christians Do
But Poor Christians Struggle With

Valerie McIntosh

THE BOOK THAT CHANGED MY LIFE:
7 Things Wealthy Christians Do But Poor Christians Struggle With
www.bookthatchangedmylife.com

Copyright © 2017 by Valerie McIntosh

Unless otherwise indicated, all Scripture quotations are taken from the Holy Bible, New Living Translation, copyright © 1996, 2004, 2007, 2013, 2015 by Tyndale House Foundation. Used by permission of Tyndale House Publishers, Inc., Carol Stream, Illinois 60188. All rights reserved.

THE HOLY BIBLE, NEW INTERNATIONAL VERSION®, NIV® Copyright © 1973, 1978, 1984, 2011 by Biblica, Inc.™ Used by permission. All rights reserved worldwide.

Scripture quotations marked NKJV are taken from The New King James Version of the Bible. Copyright © 1079, 1980, 1982 by Thomas Nelson, Inc., Publishers. Used by permission. Some passages are paraphrased for effect.

Publisher
10-10-10 Publishing
Markham, ON
Canada

ISBN: 978-1-77277-154-1

Contents

I dedicate *The Book That Changed My Life* to my lovely, intelligent, creative, barrier-breaking, and dream-building daughter, Tonia-Lee.

To Ms. Tonia-Lee McIntosh-Smith, whom we call Princess … because you simply are! Princess, I remember a few months ago you said, "Mom, you must start this book right now. Now! Just do it Mom …Do it now! You can't stop talking about it, so please, just do it! I know you're gonna eventually do it anyway!" You did not give me a chance to respond. I was pleasantly overwhelmed by your confidence in me. So, I wrote down what you said to me … And the rest was history! You had just given me a taste of what I normally dish out to you when I know you really want something and need only some motivation to go get it. I could not resist the faith you had in me. So, I stood right up and, in a few seconds, decided to sign-up to get this book done.

We both know that you are sitting on a few books, trying to make them perfect. It is now your turn. I am telling you, "Just do it! … Go publish them!"

I prayed and asked God for a baby girl (yes, I know, you are no longer a baby), and you are exactly what my life desired. I thank you for being you. I love you just the way you are, and I love the young woman you are being. You are light!

Thanks Princess!
Love always,   Mom

Acknowledgements

I am deeply honoured to have around me, family, friends, colleagues, mentors, and clients, who have made, directly or indirectly, valuable contribution to my life's journey and purpose. This book is about experience, attachment to what life has taught us, self-reflection, desire for growth and happiness, and the internal fight to decide for change toward fulfillment of our hearts' purpose as it pertains to riches or wealth. This book is written from a perspective of moving into and claiming *your* financial position, but its lessons can be easily applied to other life's areas.

I believe that every encounter with another person exposes an opportunity for us to learn. Some encounters and learning, we forget or allow them to lie dormant in the recesses of our subconscious, but there are those people who pass through or stay in our lives and leave an unexplainable impact on us.

This book is actively alive and circulating all over the world because the following individuals impacted me in such a way:

My mother, Sybil McIntosh – She is now deceased, but the world will continue to know a little bit of her through my living. Her essence remains, to me, a peaceful rock, resting actively in faith with the wealthiest heart.

Raymond Aaron – An amazing coach and New York Times bestselling author whose belief in the success of this book was contagious to me. Your knowledge and guidance made what could have been an exhausting process, easy and possible. No one does it better than Raymond!

Cara Witvoet – My personal book architect. I thank you for your encouragement, recommendations, and timely reminders.

My Siblings, Nieces & Nephews – My thoughts and desire to honour you and be an example in any way, keeps me happily motivated. I've got the best!

Garfield Bembridge – Director of Organizational Performance and Accreditation. Thanks for opportunities, respect, laughter and abundant kindness to all you come in contact with. You are a genuine prototype.

Mrs. Catherine Grossman – A sincere and understanding business woman who partnered with me during my budding business stages. I am grateful for you.

My clients – I thank you for the experience of allowing me to serve you. Cheers to the future!

Testimonials

"You taught me how to dare to reflect on my life, and especially on my limiting beliefs that I didn't even know I had. Thanks for the breakthroughs."
"Indebted Client"

"Finally, someone audacious enough to talk about the discrepancy that exists in the Christian community around worshipping the God who owns everything, while simultaneously teaching the illogical concept taught over centuries that He does not want people to be rich."
"A Non-Christian"

"If we, as adults, apply what is written in the pages of this book, we will save not only ourselves but generations from poverty and living mediocre lives. And yes, this book is for young people too. Every library and bookstore is deserving of this book."
Kinda Williams, Child & Youth Counsellor

"This book is an easy read of DEEP STUFF. The genius in the author is revealed in this book. I, personally, have been looking at the laws of the universe—like the Law of Attraction, the Law of Reciprocity, etc.—as if they were created by great teachers, like Napoleon Hill and Bob Proctor. However, this book has led me to believe that all the fundamentals of *laws of the universe* have their source in the Bible. This totally obliterates the familiar belief that being wealthy equates ungodliness, lacking in humility or living in greed. There is no excuse—go get your life!"
Teresita, Executive Coach

Foreword

You are reading a book that is unique. *The Book That Changed My Life: 7 Things Wealthy Christians Do But Poor Christians Struggle With* is the clearest expression of Valerie McIntosh. She is an amazing writer who reveals the resources of the world to you, and once you become aware of them you will then desire them badly enough to GO FOR IT! Although this book appears, at first sight, to be written for Christians, do not be deceived – whatever religious affiliation or non-religious belief system you identify with, this book is written for you!

As a Christian, you may be living a life of quiet desperation, and you may be struggling with the confusion of whether or not God wants you to attain earthly riches.

This book uses supporting evidence from the Bible to illuminate what you may already know about attracting wealth, but you most likely do not practice this even though it is stated in the Bible. This book could very well be the book that lights the fire within you towards achieving financial freedom and wealth. It does not only give you theory; it gives you lessons and reasons for practical living.

The Book That Changed My Life goes above and beyond answering your questions on subject matters such as, the rich mindset versus the poor mindset, and where all the wealth is in the world. Valerie will teach you how to, and why you should, take care of your mind, so that you can attract wealth. You will learn how to work your faith to give birth to your financial dream, and your obligation as a budding or already wealthy person.

Valerie is an award-winning author; her book delivers incredible interpretations and teachings that you will choose to grab on to as rules. You will gain clear insight to help you in your transition from poverty to wealth. If you are already wealthy, this book is definitely written to help you maintain and improve your mindset of financial and material success, while keeping you humble and powerful.

This book was written with YOU in mind!

Raymond Aaron
New York Times Bestselling Author

Bonus Chapter

YOUR JOURNEY STARTS HERE!

Why I Felt Motivated To Write This Book

I felt motivated to write this book because too many of us Christians have allowed our minds, rituals, and history to hold us back from living financially comfortable or wealthy lives. The majority of Christians I come in contact with struggle with the idea that they can have wealth and simultaneously honour God.

We have somehow allowed what we have learnt from our environment growing up to be our entire way of seeing things. We accept this history of ours to be our present. While this is not an entirely bad thing in and of itself, the problems become inherent when we start believing and owning all of our history as if we *decided* them for our lives and chose to live within their limits. We do not truly take time to reflect and see that, while everyone inherits some history, each individual has the choice and ability to change that history for better or for worse. Being complacent and living only by the history that was passed on to you is actually living below your potential and living off the work and accomplishments of others. We tend to fight to hold on to our history because to take it away feels like people are trying to strip us of who we are. So, we hold on with all our strength to what is keeping us from making progress. Your history must be used to make you stronger and better for your own self and for the world. You will never be able to live fully in your parents', foreparents', friends', pastors', or leaders' histories, because they are the ones who lived it, experienced it, and truly know it. You may choose to read about it, talk about it, remember it in detail, or try to forget all about it; but since you will never be able to see it in whole through their lens, your only obligation is to use it to take a step up and forward. If you decide to use the teachings from your history and environment that way, you will be left with taking responsibility for your own life in definite ways. When you start taking definite action on your life, you begin to automatically see life through your lens. Then questions and concerns about life become genuine to you as an individual, and your change starts happening from within that leads to both you and others being changed in the process.

It is not easy to change our minds or our views because it is part of our perceived identity and security. However, that is why the Bible says, in Romans 12:2 (NLT), "Don't copy the behavior and customs of this world, but let God transform you into a new person by changing the way you think. Then you will learn to know God's will for you, which is good and pleasing and perfect." Another version of the Bible, the NKJV, says "... be ye transformed by the renewing of your mind ..."

The above text is not to be taken lightly. Part of its message is warning us, commanding us, and directing us at the same time.

We are a part of this world, and it does not matter if we are talking about the global world, our cultural world, or our immediate community "world"—including our church world or group—or the closer world that we were born into and build with our families. The text is demanding that we do not blindly conform to these various groups. We must leave room in our minds for change. The change that is required of us is to be *transformed.* We can do that only *by the renewing of our minds.* For those of us who believe that we have put our minds under lock and key for God and that we will now allow anyone or anything to corrupt our minds, I have news for you— you are lying to yourself. As long as you are alive, events, circumstances, people, things, animals, and situations are affecting your individual mind, whether you know it or not. You have listened to the teachings of others to aid in your relationship with God. You were not born knowing all that you know, even though you "own" what you know. I think we can all agree that it is to our benefit not to leave our minds wide open to every idea and teaching that comes our way; at the same time, we must have some room in our minds for conscientious change.

With that room, you can maintain a close relationship with God and still be able to consider ideas and interpretations for better living from those whom God has placed in your world. However, because of your relationship with God, you must be ready to take what comes from your world and prove whether it is good and acceptable—in line with the will of God. There is no other way to do that than through communicating with God and studying the Holy Bible. There is simply no short-cut to ensuring that you are living a life in line with God's will, outside of spending personal, one-on-one time with the Word. Why the Word? In the beginning was the Word, and the Word was with God, and the Word was God (John 1:1, NIV). The Word is one with God! In simplest terms, spending diligent time studying the Bible with the intention of honouring Him means that you are spending quality time with God.

Wealth & Stewardship

The term stewardship means that you take care of things that are entrusted to you. Stewardship does not consist of money and money management. It is bigger than that and also includes time, talent, and relationship. However, for the purpose of this book, we will spotlight material wealth, including money and money management.

> Stewardship means that you take care of things that are entrusted to you.

So, fundamentally, we know that the wealth we have belongs to God. They are his assets, and we should strive to operate by a fiduciary standard where our first responsibility is to God, not to our individual selves. We are stewards of everything God has placed on this earth and given us dominion over.

Just as a businessman, or woman, who is responsible for people's assets in a modern day business, is paid based on how much they protect and grow these assets, it is the same way that we get rewarded for using God's assets for his cause. His cause, in simple terms, would be: for us to live fulfilling lives, to help others live better lives, and all the while, in the process, honour Him. In Deuteronomy 8:18, God tells Moses to tell the people that God will give the people the resources to make wealth in order to keep his covenant, but that the people must remember Him.

Generally, you can expect to face some kind of difficulty when managing wealth. The question is, how do you know what to fight for, transfer, or keep, if you are misusing what you have and oblivious to honouring the one who allowed you to have it in the first place. God wants to trust you with managing his wealth, and that takes an ongoing relationship of faith and discipline. That means that you have to spend time with God and in his word to know how he works and how He would prefer that you manage the particular assets in your possession.

As Christians, if you manage wealth from this view, you will struggle less with the question of whether or not God wants you to have wealth. It is never only yours, but it is placed in your hands to serve the world and be blessed in the process. You can be wealthy and not materialistic at the same time. Materialism is not a direct function of the amount of wealth you have, but it is a condition of the heart. Materialism is a desire for wealth and material possessions, with little or no desire for spiritual things. Spiritual things involve love and relationship to others, including God.

Many of us want wealth, but can we keep it in its rightful place, and are we developing ourselves in preparation for wealth? Can God trust you with a little trouble? You must choose to live daily as if you have to prove to God that whatever he entrusts you with, you can manage it. If God has ordained you for things, but it seems like every time you get close enough to lift your hands and take hold of it, something pulls it away, it could very well be a test. In times like this, God wants to have confidence in you that you will not cast the mission aside. When we give up, we are telling God that he does not know what he is doing. Sometimes, due to our fear, we knowingly, or unknowingly, sabotage our own progress toward attaining wealth, and then blame God for missed opportunities. At other times, we face a little challenge and then turn to God and say that He is giving us more than we can bear, not realizing that we are also saying that he cannot depend on us.

You and I must remember that whatever God gives us to manage for him is also meant to be a blessing for us, whether or not we can see the blessing at the time. We must endure for his assigned purpose for our lives. Some of you mope for things and, after receiving it, quit too easily. Some of you see what you ask for coming, and quit, even before taking hold of it, because you only talked loosely about wanting it and failed to prepare yourself for it.

Let's look at a story of three biblical individuals, namely Mary, Joseph, and their son, Jesus. Mary was blessed with a baby, whom she was told would save the world; but she had to run with the pregnancy, could not rest long enough to enjoy her husband, her son did not always acknowledge her as his mother and, then, after all of that, her son was crucified by some of the very people they thought loved Him. The moral of this story: Faith and dedicated performance of your life's duties do not come in the absence of fear. Faith is faith because we give it value when we choose to let it reign over our fears in spite of circumstances. Of course, we know that Jesus was eventually victorious; so, Mary and Jesus both fulfilled their visions and missions. You must have, or build, the *decision of discipline* to stick with what God entrusts you with, even when people do not understand your perspective, criticize your difficult journey, or question your faith and your relationship with Jesus. You must decide to ride it out! Really KNOW that God has put you in it to win it—so stick to it! When God puts a job in your hands, you can rest assured that he has already placed within you every bit of strength, and put in place all of the resources that you need to manage and complete that task.

Are you a Christian that wants God to bless you with money and property? You must expand your thinking—your vision. By virtue of being human, God has already made you a responsible steward of other people by solving particular problems in their lives or in their community. It is through service to others and filling their needs that we are blessed in the process. Stop expecting God to be your vending machine from space that drops items on your lap at your every demand. And sometimes we have the audacity to get upset and attempt to turn away from God when we do not receive what we demanded of Him. Do we forget? ... Everything is His! If someone treated us that way, we would think that person was out of place, would we not? Go out and solve a problem; add value to people and to the world, and the money, relationships, success, and value that you so desire, will begin to come from within you and attract more of its kind.

Who Owns It All

We just spotlighted stewardship, and now we will spotlight ownership. To understand stewardship, we must start with ownership. To understand ownership, we must start with sovereignty. To understand sovereignty, we must start with God.

"The earth is the LORD's, and everything in it" (Psalm 24:1, NIV). If you believe in this text, then you must agree that there is no room in it for you to truly own anything; meaning, you can only be a steward.

Deuteronomy 8:10-17 explains the human heart and how easy it is after we have the wealth in our possession to forget that it is God who is blessing us. God warns us to beware that we do not forget Him because, after we have the food, houses, livestock, silver, and gold, and see how they are multiplying, our hearts can easily become proud and forget that it was God who brought us out of poverty. We start to say to ourselves that "my power and the strength of my hands have produced this wealth for me" (verse 17, NIV).

Mark 10: 25 (NIV) declares: "It is easier for a camel to go through the eye of a needle than for someone who is rich to enter the kingdom of God." This does not mean that wealth is bad in and of itself, but it is because of the flaky condition of the human heart to turn away from God in times when they think they do not need him, that this text has credence.

Anything that has gotten better in your life is because God has given you the ability to do better. You could not have done better outside of God. That is why a person who confesses gratitude is naturally honouring God as the owner. This is so amazing because, by respecting God as the owner, we are also allowing Him to take responsibility for anything that is broken under our stewardship, thereby saving ourselves much distress. Remember that Satan tried to own God's company instead of being a steward and was cast out of heaven. In your heart, you must always pursue being a steward and not the final owner of what God has blessed you with. I do understand that we use the term owner to communicate in our daily interactions but, while you do so, make it a habit to remind yourself daily of who the real owner is.

Putting Wealth in Its Rightful Place

Many Christians believe that wealth is "worldly," or ungodly, because we were taught that very earlier on in life. (Remember, you read about history and environment earlier.) I recently came across a Bible study website that defined covetousness as a strong desire after the possession of worldly things. I was not in full agreement with this view because it is these general assumptions that lead people to believe that wealth is bad and that Christians must refrain from pursuing wealth in order to honour God. This type of teaching leads the majority of Christians to lead unhappy, poor, and unsatisfied lives. The majority of Christians are broke, sad, and unfulfilled. The saddest part about this is that they blame God for their situation because they believe that God does not want them to have wealth, or that God sees them as inadequate to manage his wealth, and so he is always the one who is not giving it to them.

Think about this: science and theology are the two sources where we generally look for answers to existential questions. Both of these areas support the Bible and clearly indicate that we have infinite potential. Most Christians work at a nine-to-five job on weekdays and go to church on Sabbath or Sunday, and they repeat this for their entire lifetime. No wonder some of you are so unfulfilled with your life. This clearly sounds like ritual way of living and does not, and cannot, reflect a human with infinite potential. You must feel free to explore the world, seeking your highest potential. There is nothing wrong with a nine-to-five job, but are you creative and able to function at your best there? Are you recognized for it? Is the quality of your life getting better? How much have you grown from working at this job?

Bob Proctor is a world renowned speaker. To reflect part of his speech that I once heard: money affects every area of our lives that we choose to think is important. However, after living 50 or 60 years, 90% of people are broke. It is my opinion that people have allowed their history and environment to make them live ritualistically and in denial. I say denial because everyone knows that money is imperative for living well; yet we contradict knowing that with telling ourselves that we do not need money or that money is inherently bad. How can it be inherently bad if it is a need?

Being happy, healthy, and wealthy is possible, and it should be more common than it currently is. I will always strive to stay with the group of people who are healthy, wealthy, and happy, or on their way to achieving that. I do not mean to not look after people who have less to live with due to what life has dealt them. I mean to be with dream building, life-fulfilling, and world-changing individuals who can and will, or are working to help out the less fortunate. Working and strategizing to earn more money is not an ungodly or unchristlike way of living. Think about it this way: if you are a healthy individual, you generally spend between 8 to 12 hours on your regular job, 5 to 6 days a week. That is about 40 to 72 hours in one week, or 160 to 288 hours in 1 month, or 1,920 to 3,456 hours in a single year. That is, you are spending about a third to almost half of your year in the typical pattern of working for a business where you exchange your time for money but may be unfulfilled because your life is stagnant. Now, do you think the God that you serve, and that you say you trust with your life because he "holds the world in his hands," will condemn you for choosing to use this time more efficiently? What if you learn how to use the talents, abilities, and visions you already have, to break out from your pattern of working, and into investing and networking with others to build something that is in line with your purpose? This will allow you to feel better about your relationship with God because you are using honest means to grow yourself and what you have to offer the world.

The story is told of a master who owned property, namely talents, and left his servants as stewards over portions of his property while he travelled. To do justice to this story or parable, read it below, just as it is written in the International Standard Version Bible in Matthew 8: 4-30:

"The Parable about the Talents"

"Similarly, it is like a man going on a trip, who called his servants and turned his money over to them. To one man he gave five talents, to another two, and to another one, based on their ability. Then he went on his trip.

The one who received five talents went out at once and invested them and earned five more. In the same way, the one who had two talents earned two more. But the one who received one talent went off, dug a hole in the ground, and buried his master's money. After a long time, the master of those servants returned and settled accounts with them. The one who had received five talents came up and brought five more talents. 'Master,' he said, 'you gave me five talents. See, I've earned five more talents.'

His master told him, 'Well done, good and trustworthy servant! Since you've been trustworthy with a small amount, I'll put you in charge of a large amount. Come and share your master's joy!' The one with two talents also came forward and said, 'Master, you gave me two talents. See, I've earned two more talents.'

His master told him, 'Well done, good and trustworthy servant! Since you've been trustworthy with a small amount, I'll put you in charge of a large amount. Come and share your master's joy!' Then the one who had received one talent came forward and said, 'Master, I knew that you were a hard man, harvesting where you haven't planted and gathering where you haven't scattered any seed. Since I was afraid, I went off and hid your talent in the ground. Here, take what's yours!'

His master answered him, 'You evil and lazy servant! So you knew that I harvested where I haven't planted and gathered where I haven't scattered any seed? Then you should've invested my money with the bankers. When I returned, I would've received my money back with interest.' Then the master said, 'Take the talent from him and give it to the man who has the ten talents, because to everyone who has something, more will be given, and he'll have more than enough. But from the person who has nothing, even what he has will be taken away from him. Throw this useless servant into the darkness outside!'"

Before you read any further, stop and think about the messages for you in that story.

The message of this text, in the most simplified way, is that whatever is left in your position by another should be treated with the utmost care and, where possible, be returned better than it was received. In other words, the assets are meant to grow and, most importantly, there is always an inherent reward of the growth of your inner self as a fellow human being in the process of managing the assets.

The ending of the story is meant to shock us with the extreme consequence that was meant for the steward that did not invest his master's talent. The servant was called *useless* and was cast out like waste material. The message is clear: if God puts even a minimal amount of wealth in your possession, you must manage it with the utmost care and in His best interest. In other words, you have permission to assess everything in your possession right now and look into how best you can put it to use so that it will yield its highest profit. Applying this principle will not only benefit the owner but also the person who invested it. This principle could be applied in our homes, on the job, and in our businesses. When we help others grow, we experience personal growth. It is impossible for you to help someone else without simultaneously *helping* yourself.

There is another lesson to be learnt from the middle verses of this story, where the person with the responsibility for one talent returned it with no interest but with much complaint. This servant could have asked the other servants how they were going to manage their master's talents and learn from them; instead, he chose to remain closed in his own judgments about others and in his faulty paradigms about what he thought the best way was to manage the talent.

Are you like that sometimes? Do you spend time criticizing individuals with money instead of managing whatever little is in your possession? Is it possible that you are retarding your own growth of wealth by creating your own limits from judging others and falsely assuming that your boss or business partner, or your God, wants you to refrain from investing and networking? God created us to be builders and not destroyers. When you work or meet with someone in any capacity, the person must be left elevated to some degree.

You must not compare your possessions with anyone else's. This kind of thinking and behaviour will cause you to feel lesser in value than others who have more than you. Wealth has a rightful place in each person's life, as long as that person is multiplying it to bless themselves and others honourably. Stop worrying about what other people do with what God gave them, and worry about what you are doing with what God has given you!

> Stop worrying about what other people do with what God gave them,
> and worry about what you are doing with what God has given you!

You must realize that the servant who was responsible for 5 talents, returned 10 talents as a result of investing them. The servants responsible for 2, returned 4, and for the same reason. Both servants presented a 100% return on their talents despite the different quantities that were entrusted to them. Because they managed their master's talents with best inventions, they were invited to share in the master's joy and entrusted with more talents. On the other hand, the possession of the stingy servant was transferred over to the servant who already controlled the majority of the talents.

This helps answer the question that people have: Why do the rich get richer and the poor get poorer? Some of the reasons for this is that when you have a little bit of wealth, you look around and compare how much other people have and become scared that you may lose what you have. But you soon realize that the more you squeeze and tightly control the little wealth or money you have, the more it slips away. Why? Because you are acting out of fear, and fear constricts and destroys people, relationships, and things, including wealth.

Be fearless but diligent in investing the little money that you have—make your money wisely make more money for you, and see how much more wealth will come your way.

Covetousness and Jealousy

Covetousness and jealousy can hinder us from developing our minds in a healthy way for preparation to receive, manage, and share what God has for us.

Covetousness is the active state that a person experiences when they strongly desire something that belongs to someone else. Covetousness does not only involve money, cars, and houses but also relationships, intelligence, and professions.

One way to gauge if you are currently being covetous is to genuinely ask yourself, or someone close to you, if it is ever observed that you are satisfied and grateful with what you already have. Then, take necessary actions to make gratefulness a normal part of your daily life.

We allow covetousness to happen so passively within us, as if it does not have harmful results. When you become covetous of someone else's property, you are depleting your self-worth. You are also blocking wealth from coming your way because you begin to think about the other person as more deserving than you. You are also associating negative thoughts and emotions to wealth or whatever else you are jealous of. Your subconscious mind does not distinguish that your energy is only directed to the wealth of someone else and not to other sources of wealth, so it sets you up to move away from wealth. Your subconscious mind, in doing so, thinks that it is protecting you from something that makes you upset and unhappy. Additionally, when you spend your energy in such a negative way on others, you cheat yourself from using it positively toward your own goals.

If your attitude toward people who have more wealth than you is covetous and lustful, it will be revealed through your words. Your words can raise you up or damn you. You may begin to think and say that the person with wealth is trusting in material things instead of God or that they may have gained it by some dishonest means, when that could be furthest from the truth. In your attempt to judge other people's relationships with their wealth against their relationship with God, you are bound to end up judging others unfairly. That is not the kind of effect you would want to have on the world if you want to grow as an individual and grow your wealth, which demands a healthy relationship with others who have either more or less than you.

Jealousy is the feeling of unhappiness and anger that you experience when someone has something or someone that you want. This literally means that you believe that you are more deserving of what that person has than them.

Operating under the spirit or energy of covetousness and jealousy is not of God. The spirit of God is the Holy Spirit. Therefore, covetousness and jealousy is not from a place of love, kindness, abundance, gratitude, and inner peace.

Jealousy can cause you to become angry, hateful, envious, and discouraged, and can lead to ruining potentially good relationships. In fact, some of you may remember a time when you created strife or changed a good relationship between you and someone else, not because the other person hurt you but because you created a whole scenario in your head about the other person, or a scenario of what you believed that person was thinking toward you. Either way, this thinking or energy is destructive.

Thinking that others are always jealous of you can also cause you to falsely believe that you are better than others. Whether you are on the giving or receiving end of covetousness and jealousy, you are retarding your personal growth because, instead of spending time on learning from the person that you are jealous of, or giving to the person whom you believe is jealous of you, you use your time thinking unpleasant thoughts toward that person. Proverbs 23:7 (KJV) says: "For as he thinketh in his heart, so *is* he." In other words, all of the negative and unhealthy thoughts that you hold toward others is, in reality, in your heart, meaning that you are disturbing your own inner peace and cheating yourself of experiencing your own true value as the good person God intended you to be. Such was the case of the man called King Saul, in the Bible. He developed such jealousy and focused so much of his energy on David that it led to his own fatal self-destruction. This story can be found in the Bible in 1 Samuel 18:1-30; 19:1-18.

(After answering the activity questions for this section that can be found on www.bookthatchangedmylife.com) If you identify as someone who has experienced, or is experiencing, jealousy, please know that it is more common than people would admit, and every single person has experienced it at one time or another.

This is part of our fallen nature. Countries are sometimes jealous of other countries; campuses within particular schools are often jealous of the other; churches are sometimes jealous of other churches…and the list goes on.

In order to get over jealousy and covetousness, you must know that God has enough of everything for everyone to share. The Bible, in James 4: 5-6, tells us that God is aware of the envy and pride that is in us but that he gives greater grace so that we can live a life that does not harbor envy and pride. It says God opposes the arrogant but gives grace to the humble. That is why Christians must see themselves as stewards and not ultimate owners of what God entrusts to us. This perspective helps free our minds to see that others can share in the abundance of this universe.

You must understand and know in your heart that the world is abounding in what other people have that you are jealous of. Other people's wealth does not limit the amount of what is available to you. In Psalm 37, David says that we should not fret or be jealous of others who seem to have it all, especially when we say we are trusting in the Lord. With wealth comes great responsibility. Again, focus on using what you already have to honour God, and you will see your increase in due time. If God wants you to have what others have, he will give you what others have. I like how, in Isaiah 60: 5, God says to the Israelites that their hearts will throb and swell with joy because he will direct wealth from others to them. Read it yourself! Why would anyone not be honourable in the way they manage the portion of wealth that is in their possession if they *really* knew to whom it belongs and who has ultimate control over it?

There is no room for God's children to be spending their valuable days, weeks, months, or years in jealousy of others. It is not our place to take inventory of where others get their wealth from. Consider these two options: if others are accumulating their wealth through unfair means, the Bible commands us in Psalm 37 that we must not fret [or be jealous/envious] of those who do evil or wrong because, like the grass and green plants, they will soon wither and die away. You are asked to trust in the Lord and do well, without comparing yourself to anyone else, and He will bring your wishes to pass and give you the desires of your heart.

Here is why the majority of wealthy people are not jealous of poor or even rich people: they know that they have acquired the wisdom to rebuild almost any material thing that is lost. Henry Ford, establisher of the Ford Motor Company, once said, *"You can take my factories, burn up my buildings, but give me my people and I'll build the business right back again."* Practice spending your time learning how to build wealth instead of looking at others with jealous or covetous eyes and reasoning.

There is one more thing I must share, especially for the benefit of young people: Do not indulge in using your parents' or guardians' wealth as though it were yours. By all means, share of it and enjoy it as you are allowed, because it is in your family. It is a blessing. However, do not indulge in spending your parents' hard earned money frivolously, or use their expensive cars to show off to your friends as if they were actually yours. This kind of thinking and behaving will be sure to stunt your growth and your individual achievements in life by deceiving you into thinking that you have more than you actually do. You must work as hard as you can in a healthy way to build on top of what your family already has. It is vain to boast in another man's labour. I also know women who are stuck in life because they only lavished in their husband's growth, only to later get divorced. Although 2 Corinthians 10: 15-16 is written in a different context in the Bible, I believe I can safely use it to elucidate this point. It talks about not boasting of things without measure, that is, of other people's labours, but having hope, when your faith is increased, that you shall be enlarged as you continue to perform your duties and increase your faith in the process because this is according to God's rule of abundance. It continues to remind us not to boast in another man's [or woman's] line of things made ready to our hands or made available for our use.

Developing and maintaining the habit of enjoying the possessions of others as if they were yours can contribute to you missing out on your own calling in life, or at least delay the process. We need each other, but let us keep things in our relationships in their respective places so that we can rise creatively and optimally.

So, now that you know that your relationship and attitude toward God, others, and wealth reflects the kind of person you are, and the quality of your life's journey to attaining things, I hope you will *choose* to be the best you can in those areas.

The next chapter will introduce you to the power of your mind, remind you that you have control of your mind, and use comparisons to share how your mindset can affect the quality and quantity of what you get in life.

I have placed an activity workbook on the book's website. You may go onto the website and download it. As you read to the end, in most cases, of each chapter. I urge you to do the short activities from the workbook. It will help you personalise and apply some of the contents in each chapter.

The workbook valued at $37.00 is my free gift to you.

Chapter 1

DOES THE MIND REALLY EXIST?

Distinguishing the Mind and the Brain

You do not have to be a science major to know what the brain is. It is now common knowledge that the brain is a three pound, convoluted mass of gray and white matter inside our skull that serves to organize, synchronize, and control our psychological and physiological processes.

It is not so easy to speak about the mind. As far as I know, there has been no single agreed upon definition that fully captures what the mind truly is. In fact, more and more research and individual experiences are revealing the uncontainable vastness and potential yet uniqueness of the human mind.

The psychiatric and medical professions, although extensions of the same fundamental work, have their own varying functional definitions of the mind. A prominent doctor, Dr. Dan Siegel, coined the term "mindsight" to describe the human capacity to see the internal workings of our minds and also perceive the minds of others. He explains that our ability to understand our own minds helps us get ourselves off of the autopilot of ingrained behaviors and habitual responses, meaning that it allows us to "name and tame" the emotions and thoughts we are experiencing, rather than choosing to remain in a state of being overwhelmed by them. (You will see more of the importance of this when we discuss paradigms.)

Mind-Health

It is not possible to experience personal growth and progress with *sustained success* in your Christian life, which is your everyday living, without renewing your mind. The Bible says "renew*ing*" of your mind (in Romans 12:2) because it is an ongoing process— it is definitely not a one-time-thing. The day you think that your mind has made it, and it does not need improvement, change, growth, or renewing, is the day you, as a person, start to die, spiritually and otherwise in your daily living.

Now, because as Christians your foundation is God, you must believe in the renewing of your minds. The only way to renew your minds, which is basically exchanging your thoughts for His way of thinking, is through studying His Word. Consequently, if you have stopped spending time in the Word—the Holy Bible— with an open mind, it also means that you are leaving your mind open to bondage or ungodly, selfish thinking. Your thoughts control your life! It doesn't take much analyzing to figure out that if you are not conscientiously thinking about your thoughts, you will, by default, end up doing what you did not mean to do and not doing what you prefer to do. Even when you think you know what it is you are supposed to do, the pressures of your environment and of life in general can quietly skew our thoughts, and hence our actions, taking us in a direction where we never wanted to go and making us into a person we never thought we would become. It is fundamentally important to take a few seconds randomly over the course of each day to pay attention to where your mind has drifted and dwelled on. Get into the practice immediately of redirecting and changing your thought contents to what you want them to be.

Rich Mind. Poor Mind

A rich-minded or wealthy-minded person normally overlooks the benign shortcomings of others and instead focuses on finding purpose from what others' lives are teaching. On the contrary, when poor-minded individuals dislike something about another person, they tend to withdraw entirely from that person and deny themselves from learning anything else that person or the situation has to offer. Rich-minded Christians are telling you the tools that they are using to get rich, and you, with your poor mindedness, are standing by criticizing them; most times, not for doing anything illegal, unethical, or ungodly, but simply because they are rich, and you do not know how they got there. Your poor mind is telling you that you are in such a rut and there is no way you can get out of it, so, subconsciously, you are also telling yourself that the people who got out of their poor situations must have had to do something ungodly, unethical, or dishonest to have their better lives.

People who were poor, but got out of their poverty to a life of plenty, had to work their way out of their poverty mindset, especially if they wanted to hold on and manage the wealth they got.

Poor people need to listen to the stories of wealthy people who share similar values but got out of poverty, instead of just having this general mental block toward the entire wealthy population. Most people who are wealthy are ready and willing to share their stories and their resources with those who are poor but who really want to get out of poverty.

I do not know about you, but I have met many other wealthy people who are proud to share their story and resources to help others become wealthy. Conversely, have you ever met a poor person who is proud and ready to share their story of how they were born or otherwise got into poverty, and then use their story to help others stay in poverty? To take it a bit further, who will, in their right mind, sign up for a seminar or course on how to remain or get into poverty? ...No one, because it will not add value to people's lives. I know it sounds silly to write that. The point is, if your story is one that you are not proud of, change it! How do you begin to change your story? ...By guarding your open mind to receive knowledge for growth and renewing that which is in line with God's words. Use your attitude and mindset toward others wisely.

Some Christians see the word *guard*, and they think it means *close*. If your mind is closed, that only means that you are not honouring God because you already believe that you have become perfect and leave no room for growth, even to become more Christlike.

Not poor people necessarily, but *poor minded* people are spectators as rich minded people work, strategize, gain wealth, and keep moving on. Poor minded people have that same attitude toward God. They pray and ask God to change their minds or to bless them with wealth, but they do not take action. They feel helpless about the thoughts they are having, and they feel helpless about taking action toward attaining wealth through strategic working.

The mind of a wealthy person is constantly geared on how to make their money make more money for them, whereas the mind of a poor person is generally focused on how to work or give up more hours for a few dollars. Wealthy people's money is generally an expression of themselves, whereas poor people believe money will give them an identity. Wealthy people invest in other people with the expectation of a positive outcome from whom or what they invest in, such as a neighbourhood, school, etc., whereas poor people have this false belief that they must *give away* the little gains that they have without ever expecting anything in return. Wealthy people are always endeavoring to increase in higher knowledge by tapping into what others know, whereas poor people mainly chat, fuss, or complain about their poverty, and try to find new ways of remaining on the same level from what they and others in their similar situation know, without tapping into the support of others who know how to get out.

Wealthy people create intellectual property—they take time to write down their wisdom. In other words, it moves from intellectual knowledge that can eventually belong to anyone outside of their heads, to intellectual property that can be sold to make them more wealth. Intellectual property can sell outside of you and does not require you to be laboring by the hour, day in and day out. Poor people seem to be adept at thinking-up ways that require them to be laboring away. Since they can only "split" themselves in so many ways, they limit themselves to making money only when they are physically working, and hence from earning more money or generating more wealth.

Many poor Christians see wealthy Christians as their problem and sometimes the reason for them being poor. But I challenge you to consider that wealthy people are not your main problem, and certainly not to the magnitude that you think; they are merely the conduit for conflict that you are experiencing within yourself in the spiritual realm, because you are stuck at not having what they have already attained. This internal conflict is frustrating for many struggling individuals because they do not currently see how to get out of their poverty, or how someone who has gotten out, did get out. Despite this, you must get yourself to hold on to the thought that you too can achieve more than you have and be at a better place in life.

Chapter Two will take you deeper into how your way of thinking is either contributing to your moving closer to wealth or keeping you busy trying to get out of, but stuck shuffling around in, poverty. This chapter will encourage you to do some introspection.

Valerie's Infinity Note: Wealthy Christians *spend much of their time purposefully* stimulating their minds and focusing on packaging their ideas that work, as well as creating intellectual property that builds their brands, which sends them further up the wealth ladder.

Activity Time: Download workbook (value $37) for free. www.bookthatchangedmylife.com

Chapter 2

DISTORTED THINKING & PARADIGMS

What Is A Paradigm?

A *Paradigm* is a collection of thought patterns, behaviors, and perceptions that dictate your feelings, actions, and results. To change your paradigm, you have to do it intentionally; it does not happen by default, and you cannot do it passively.

Unhealthy paradigms, which is referred to in everyday transformational speaking language, is not different from the term *distorted thinking,* which I often use in therapy sessions with clients, or a form of what is referred to in the Bible as *strongholds.* I use them interchangeably here. A stronghold is a mindset that holds you hostage against rising with the potential that God has for your life. Distorted thinking and paradigms are processed in the mind. You must come against them as if you were fighting a spiritual warfare, because that is what this intangible thing that has the ability to control your mind is.

James 4: 5-6, a text previously referred to, makes it easier for us to take action toward attaining wealth because the text is also saying that if God placed wealth in our hands, that whatever difficulties in mindset or external circumstances that might show up, God has GREATER grace; that is, grace that is greater than the difficulties. The real problem, for some of you, is that you keep yourself stuck in your limiting mindset because it truly feels like your current way of thinking is somehow protecting you. Of course, if something is perceived as a protection, it will feel right; as a result, you block off even better opportunities and ways of thinking that challenge your current mindset, and you remain stuck in the very situation, relationship, etc., that you want to get out of. Job 22: 29 shows how God dealt with a man named Job in the Bible. Job was a humble, healthy and wealthy man but life situations happened to him and he lost all of his wealth. The Bible says that when Job was cast down (going through this rough time), he spoke with confidence about how all that he had belonged to God and how he will serve God with or without material wealth, even in his poor physical health. Yes, Job said that even if God withdrew his blessing from him and left him broke and sick, that he would still honour God as God. For Job to honour God in this way, he had to surrender his way of thinking and all human forms of security for a while, and rest in promise of, and power of, someone who knew better than Him. He did not shut out others totally; he also welcomed their opinions but rejected practicing some of them because they were not in line with honouring God. As a result, God saved him from dying from the physical ailments he was experiencing at the time and restored all of the wealth he had, plus more—God saw Job's confidence in Him as Humility.

Humility (open-mindedness to listen to others, then lining up your way of living with God) is Godly power! James 4:10 (ESV) commands us to "Humble yourselves before the Lord and He will exalt you."

In business, we say the first step in transformation is the transaction. In other words, after the client invests in your offer—the transaction—the transformation can happen because they can use the product or service to help change their lives. Similarly, life transformation from distorted thinking and unhealthy paradigms can only truly happen after the transaction. The good news is that the main transaction has already taken place. It took place when Jesus gave his life in exchange for you to be restored unto him eternally. Now, you only need to claim what He has promised you in the Bible, and claiming it does not only mean naming it; you must also believe it or live your life like you know without a shadow of a doubt that the promises will come through because of who gave them.

Let us reflect briefly again on Romans 12:2 (KJV): "...but be ye transformed by the renewing of your mind ...." Meriam-Webster's dictionary defines transform as: to change in composition or structure; to change the outward form or appearance of; to change in character or condition. When the Bible tells us that we must be "transformed," the Bible is plainly and unequivocally telling us that we must make a paradigm shift in order to line up with what the *good, acceptable*, and *perfect* will of God is for our lives. It is saying to experience change in whatever fundamentally makes you up, such as the values, ideals, thought patterns and points-of-view you hold, your physical appearance and the presence you emanate, or your character and internal or external condition or situation. Then it goes on to say that the only way you can achieve that is by the renewing your mind, which is the way to prove that what you are doing is within what is good and acceptable.

You have not made a paradigm shift, or you are not transformed from your distorted thinking, if you are having the same thoughts and doing all of the same things you used to do with the same old people or group, in the same old environment, that do not contribute to you living a fulfilling life. As a Christian, you might be praying repeatedly to God. God is willing and ready to answer you, but your mindset could be preventing you from seeing a path to the answer, all because you have allowed yourself to be locked into your old mindset.

A paradigm is basically a stronghold, as termed in the Bible and stated above, and a stronghold is simply a lie that you believe, consciously or unconsciously, as a result of a significant experience or accumulation of experiences. The fact remains that you are living within the limitations of this internal fence.

Are You Aware of Your Distorted Thinking & Paradigms?

Every human being lives with the influence of others on them. As we become adults, we have the right and freedom to question the programming that has been placed in us from our environments.

Have you convinced yourself that life is not going to get any better for you, and this is as good as it gets? You should often pay attention to your thoughts. Know that this is where you are but not where you will be. You must reprogram your thinking in order to break out of generations or major events that got you to where you are. Know that you can rise above poverty and mediocrity, but you *must* challenge your way of thinking. In terms of becoming financially free, some of you may have told yourselves that life is over for you, whilst some of you act and think like that but do it more covertly. Either way, your mentality is holding you back from a better life. Do not give up on your dreams—risk changing your mind for the better.

Another way you might have allowed your thinking to hold you back is when you rationalized and analyzed so much on a single move you wanted to take toward your goal, that you became paralyzed with fear. What happened is that you spent too much time in the *how* and caused it to overshadow your *why*. Ultimately, you still are where you started and most likely with greater fear of moving forward. When you fail to take action due to fear, you do not get the results you envisioned; that, then, weakens your faith in your thinking about your ability to succeed at the task, and you then begin to analyze, trying to find safety and certainty before making your next move…and the cycle continues.

Metacognition

Proverbs 4: 23 (NLT) basically warns us to be careful how we think because our lives are shaped by the thoughts we harbor deep inside of us. It states, "Guard your heart above all else, for it determines the course of your life." This text is beautiful; it is telling us that we have the potential and are capable of monitoring our thoughts. We are put in charge of guarding our hearts and our minds; and that means that we get to determine when to open, restrict, or close the access and contents of our minds, or manage what has already gotten into our minds. In other words, we are capable of thinking about our thoughts—Metacognition. How powerful and freeing!

After over ten plus years of practicing coaching, counseling, and psychotherapy, I witnessed one of the most unfortunate events from another clinician in the history of my role. I was present while a mutual client shared a concern with his psychiatrist who was managing his medications at the time. The client expressed that he had some significant negative thoughts over the past days. Immediately, and before assessing the client's situation further, that doctor told the client: "Well, I would not worry about it too much. Hopefully, the medication should take that away. Thoughts just come, and we do not have much control over it." Then, the client asked the doctor if there was anything else he could do to lessen the frequency and intensity of those thoughts; to which the doctor told the client, there was nothing the client could do about it.

I could tell the client was shocked, as was I. The client replied, "Really? Oh!" After the psychiatrist was gone, I asked the client, if he had some level of control over having more pleasant thoughts, what would he do? The client said, "Well, first, I think I wouldn't use as much weed [cannabis] as I did on the weekend and earlier this week." The client smiled. He realized that he had his own answer and could significantly help manage his own thoughts by managing the substances that he put into his body.

Similar to this client's situation, you have more control over your thoughts than you might like to know and take responsibility for. If you choose what you watch on television and on YouTube, and choose what quality of conversations you engage in, as well as choosing to be kind and forgiving verses revengeful and holding on to wrongs others have done to you, make no mistake, you are deciding what you think. I understand that sometimes thoughts seem to come from "nowhere" and land in your mind, but you might want to do something about them before they take root. (I also understand that, due to chemical imbalances in the brain, some individuals have struggles with their thoughts and minds. You should seek help for that, too.)

We rarely say, what's *in* your mind; we say, what's *on* your mind. "*On* your mind" gives you power to "brush off" or deal with certain things that come to your awareness. Some thoughts are not yet in your mind, or an integral part of your mind, until you allow them to become that, and by which time it becomes more difficult to train yourself out of such unhealthy thinking patterns; yet training or practicing your way out of it is very possible.

As a psychotherapist, I am very well aware of the fact that *disease*, or psychopathology, develops within some people, and therapy (talk or medication) may be the best way to jump-start or maintain the efficient working of such states of mind. In such cases, please do what your doctor recommends. At the same time, do not become lazy about what you allow in your mind and how long you allow certain unwanted or unpleasant thoughts and images to play around in your mind. The only exception would be for the purpose of exploring productive solutions toward important problems. Pay attention to your thoughts. Do not give root to or linger on evil thoughts—thoughts that do not serve your higher purpose.

Unless you are an individual who experiences severe mental health problems, and are medically out of touch with reality, do not believe anyone who tells you that you do not have any control over your own thoughts. Ecclesiastes 10:2, paraphrased, says that wise thinking leads to right living, and stupid thinking leads to wrong living. This means that you have the power to choose the quality of thoughts you maintain, consequently changing your life.

In its most fundamental way, Metacognition is a command. It *means: notice what you are noticing!* This diligent action, done periodically, can significantly change your life for the better.

What You Do Not Know Is Hurting You

Excuses, void reasons, and avoidance, most times, becomes preparation for you to return to the same old way of thinking and living.

God's words and his principles are not meant to keep his people in bondage. We should not present that to the rest of the world. God's word brings knowledge, wisdom, freedom, peace, and life. You must ask yourself, "Is my current situation what Jesus died on the cross to give me? Is the life I'm living what I believe God wants for me?" If you believe that God wants you to have a better life, then work for that better life.

Your money reflects your life's labour. Ask yourself if what you say you are doing with your money, and what you are actually doing with it, are congruent. Every Christian should have a budget. How else would you see how you are spending your money? In other words, how are you using the earthly reward of your life's work?

I know about the prosperity gospel and all of that stuff, but wealth is often a sign of spirituality. In the Book of Genesis, Chapter 13 of the Bible, we see that Abram (Abraham) became rich, and then very rich in livestock, silver, and gold, all because of his relationship with God. And, in Genesis 26:12, we find that Isaac became *very* rich because the Lord blessed him. Boaz also was very rich, and Boaz was an honourable man. In 2 Chronicles 1:11-12, Solomon asked God for wisdom and knowledge to rule the people and, because of his humility in putting the interest of the people before his personal gain (not needs), God blessed him with riches, possessions, and honour (fame). Proverbs 13:22 says that a good man leaves an inheritance to his grandchildren, and the wealth of sinners is stored up for the righteous. Yes, the Bible does say that wealth belongs to the righteous! So, if you are a Christian, put in your portion of the work, pay attention to the excuses you make that keep wealth from finding you, honour God, and watch your own life increase!

Generational Issues and Curses

Is there such a thing as *generational curses*?!

I decided to discuss generational issues, or curses, because I have come across far too many individuals, in my church network and in my professional life, who believe that some curse from their parents or grandparents was passed down to them. As a result, they believe that they are "stained for life" and are rendered helpless to change their own lives for the better.

Exodus 20:5 (KJV) states that "You shall not bow down yourself to them, nor serve them; for I, the LORD your God, *am* a jealous God, visiting the iniquity of the fathers on the children to the third and fourth *generation* of them that hate me; and showing mercy to thousands of them that love me, and keep my commandments."

This passage is not *simply* saying that God will punish the great grandchildren for the isolated sins of their great grandfathers or grandmothers. This text demonstrates that children generally practice what their parents practice. That is understandable, as parents create and shape their children's environment. In light of that, children generally practice the healthy and unhealthy behaviours that they modeled from their home environment. The Bible is saying that if, as the children grow up, *they* also continue in the unhealthy, sinful, or illegal ways of their parents, then *they* too will be visited with the consequences that their parents were visited with. To ensure that this is understood, let's step away from the Bible and apply a general, real life situation. If a father or mother is a thief, and their child grows up to be a thief as a result of his environment, that child will have to serve his time in jail or pay the consequences for stealing when he is found out. Then, if this child in turn has a child without correcting his ways, that child would likely grow up in his generation to become a thief, which will bring punishment. In other words, the grandchild has "inherited" the "curse" or sin of the grandfather, if that sin was not identified and corrected along the way. Similarly, a grandfather who grew up to be an outstanding citizen because he modeled that from his parents, will reap the benefits of this lifestyle and, most likely, so will his child and grandchild. So, the Bible is pointing to: if the iniquities of the grandfather are still on the son, and on that son's son, God will still visit them with the consequence of their chosen actions. God is not punishing the son and grandson for the sins of their father and grandfather, but God is visiting the sin, or the unhealthy behavior, the generations continue to practice.

God also said that if any of these individuals change their behaviour, that he will show mercy to them. From a real life perspective, we can say that a court judge's role is not to target and punish people, but that judge will have to lay down consequence for the person's bad behaviour. In a court of law, ignorance of the law does not excuse your breaking of the law. The judge will also likely show mercy for those individuals whose environments or family history contributed to their plight, but they are showing awareness of their bad behaviour and making even the smallest changes for the better.

Ezekiel 18: 4, 14-17 informs us that if a child of a bad parent walks his own path of a good life, then that child will not be punished for the sins or wrong doings of his father. In fact, in verse 4, God says all souls are his, and it is only the soul that continues to live in sin that will be punished.

> # You choose to be who you are
> # by the choices you make.

You choose to be who you are by the choices you make! You may have grown up in a great home with wonderful parents who were positive role models for you, but you allowed your peers from school, work, or other social environments to shape you into an unproductive lifestyle.

So, once again, you choose to be who you are by the choices you make.

I hope and pray that you feel free to change your thought patterns, behaviour, weight, financial status, job or business, or anything else that you want to improve in your life, regardless of whether your parents or grandparents were productive citizens. By God's grace, you can *walk your own* path. "For I know the plans I have for you," declares the LORD, "plans to prosper you and not to harm you, plans to give you hope and a future," Jeremiah 29:11 (NIV). God created you with purpose for your life and wants you to be excellent in your own walk. You must not allow what someone else has done, or even a mistake that you have done in the past, to get in the way of your moving forward and living an amazing life.

Just like it is difficult for anyone to allow others to love them more than they love themselves, you will find it very difficult, or even impossible, to grow in wealth beyond how much you love yourself, because receiving wealth gracefully means that you must see yourself worthy of it and be grateful for it. There is no fixed cost to your worth—your value is *life*, which has no "$" number on it—and life is worth *everything*. Love yourself, forgive yourself, and begin to see yourself as a worthy, productive person. Focus on the bigger vision of yourself that you can grow into and become.

My Prosperity Does Not Mean Your Poverty

This concept of *when another person becomes more prosperous, you become poorer*, is based in fear, not in love and abundance.

My becoming wealthy is not what is keeping you or another person poor. Christians must begin to see that one Christian's wealth could actually mean another Christian's betterment, and not the contrary. You must come from a place of abundance to understand this concept. As a Christian, if you truly believe that God owns everything, it should not be too difficult understand that his love and wealth is never ending and always available.

Direct your attention and *your* way of living to God instead of giving rise to negative energy within yourself from looking at what others have. Your *source* is God. Chapter three will speak to your heart, because it delves into that in an impactful way.

Valerie's Infinity Note: Wealthy Christians are aware that there is such a thing called paradigms, or distorted thinking. However, they do not spend their time cowering under paradigms. Instead, they *create a support team, or mastermind group, and develop better friendships and collegiality* with individuals who they know can help them strengthen these weaker areas, or get the job done for them that their less developed areas of expertise do not allow them to execute well enough. They use perceived "inherited curses" or faulty history as motivation to step out of poverty and create personal victory, and a "wowed" life, for themselves and for the benefit of others.

Activity Time: Download workbook (value $37) for free.
www.bookthatchangedmylife.com

Chapter 3

FAITH & SPIRIT

It Begins With You

The things that you are afraid of, you believe in. That is why you generally do not succeed when you are working toward something that you prefer to have but simultaneously keep repining about another thing that you might lose in the process.

Your subconscious mind causes you to see all sorts of challenges along the way that you would otherwise have not seen, in order to protect you from losing that other thing. You subconsciously sabotage your own success and then find very sincere sounding excuses in external things or people, for not succeeding. When you thought you had enough faith to attain something, which you attempted but failed at and gave up on, the reason for your final failed attempt is rarely due to external circumstances. Your failure generally happens because your faith in success throughout the process of working on that goal was not maintained in the forefront of your mind as strongly as your subconscious belief in the possibility that you will fail by losing something else. Since it may be true that attaining one thing might actually mean losing or disrupting the relationship you have with something or someone else, the body does what is simpler—it chooses to do by default what it is already familiar with. That is why you keep attracting the same old opportunities, people, and situations that you do not want, over and over again.

One smart person said that failure is the opportunity to begin again more intelligently. **Faith embraces courage, endurance, and surrender.** Your belief in your purpose or goals must be so saturated that you sometimes have to refresh your position to have a good look at what the norm is for you in a particular situation; then, deliberately practice directing your thoughts, questions, behaviours, and other specific actions toward where you want to go. You cannot afford to operate casually. Be intentional, and put your purpose above your normal way of being and above immediate desires. Faith is not casual. Faith requires change— change in your internal habits and in your behaviour.

Faith's Power Is in Its Source

The power of your faith is in the source of whom or what you place your faith in. Faith in itself has no power; it is just a word. The all-knowing God placed within us the ability to think, visualize, hope, plan, execute, and grow. Then He topped that up by having a never-ending amount of faith available for us to use at our disposal. So, faith is what it is, in the amount that it is in, and has the potential that it has, all because of whom it is from— an omnipotent creative God! So, when you take action and become creative in designing your life, you are automatically tapping into God's power that is activated as faith. That is why placing your faith in something or someone is a choice. Placing your faith in things, people, or concepts may yield results, but I declare that the greatest source of faith is God. Why? ...Because God is unchangeable. People may change their perspective on God because of their life's experience, but God does not change. God is *the* only true *source.* Whether you decide to rely on Him or not is totally up to you and is a whole new story on its own. So, your faith, basically, is your depth of reliance, belief, trust, and inner knowing of Source. Each man is given a measure of faith (Romans 12: 3). Again, what you do with that measure is up to you.

Some of you sit back and say that your faith is not strong enough. Well now, the Bible did not say that each man has been given all of the faith they will ever need. It says you are only given a measure. A measure is part of a whole; is it not? As you use the measure that you are given to its fullest capacity, guess what? It does not end there; you do not run out of faith. Instead, it takes you as a person to a higher level, closer to your goal, and your faith is naturally increased in the process. After you saturate a *measure* of your faith, you acquire more faith naturally as you move forward on your journey of increasing difficulties. Faith is in endless and infinite abundance in our universe. It is available to all in as much quantity and quality as we would like to use it and, still, there is more of it. Faith is spiritual, miraculous, and powerful; it is not for cowards and quitters. This is not meant to be an insult; it is meant to make you do some self-reflection. Really, how can you say that insufficient faith is responsible for your not taking a leap into changing your life, when faith is always available and is activated, or works only as you act forward? The reason it was insufficient is because *you* did not use it—*you* did not take action.

Discussion of faith takes me back to three stories or parables of the Bible, namely The Talents, The 10 Maidens, and The Farmer. In the first parable, which was previously used under "Bonus Chapter," three servants were each given a measure of talents—five, two, and one, respectively. The first and second servants, who were given 5 and 2 talents, both brought in 100% of their return to their boss. They doubled what they were given and returned 10 and 4 talents to him. The third servant, who did not stretch his faith to take the risk of investing his boss's talent, returned the single talent without interest and just as it were given to him. Due to this servant's limiting mindset and behaviour, his talent was taken away from him along with his other privileges, and he was forbidden from ever returning to his boss's place. In fact, he was condemned.

The Parable of The 10 Maidens or young women: These women were awaiting a bridegroom. The bridegroom had a delay. While he delayed, all of the women slept. Then there was a noise—the bridegroom arrived. All 10 of the women had taken oil lamps with them, but only 5 took vessels with extra oil. The other 5 maidens woke up to realize the bridegroom had arrived, but their lamps had used all the oil they contained. Now, the latter 5 women begged and pleaded with the other 5 women to share the oil they brought in their vessels with them, but they were denied.

Some of you use your faith like the Five Foolish Maidens, as they are called. You have a never ending faith reserve available to you, but you tend to tap into only a small amount of it. You do not even pay attention to the reserve because you think you can continue to get all of what you want to achieve from that small amount that fits your immediate situation. Then, when the time comes to use more than your typical amount of faith, you try to rely on others to carry you on theirs. Some of you even go as far as calling others selfish if they decide not to share.

You can guess how the story ends: the five young women who brought additional oil in vessels went to dine with the bridegroom; whereas, the five foolish women's journey/dream ended, not when they decided it would end but when their oil (faith) burnt up. I would not be surprised if the Five Foolish Maidens also blamed the oil for burning up so quickly instead of acknowledging that they did not assess their situation and/or prepare enough for their mission.

When you plan to attain a goal, always secure more resources than you think you will need to get the results of that goal. This story or parable brings two common sayings to mind: "If you fail to plan, you plan to fail" and "it is better to be prepared for an opportunity and not have one than to have an opportunity and not be prepared" (the latter by Whitney Young Jr.).

The third parable is of a man who is a householder and went out early in the morning to find labourers to work in his vineyard. He found some workers early that morning, and they negotiated that the owner would pay them one penny for the day's work. Then, the owner went back out three hours later and found more workers for the vineyard. They agreed that the owner would give them whatever he thinks is right to pay them. Again, the owner went out on the sixth hour, then on the ninth hour, and again on the eleventh hour. After the day's work was done, the owner called his stewardess and asked her to pay each of the workers for their day's work. All of the workers were each paid one penny. When the workers who started the job earlier in the morning saw that those who started later got the same pay as them, they became discontented and questioned why they did not receive more money than those who started later, even though they got the pay that *they* agreed on with their boss.

One lesson I draw out of this parable is to know your worth even in tough times so that you do not end up settling for less out of desperation.

Another lesson is to not compare your returns with others because you will always be dissatisfied.

One more lesson is the cliché sounding phrase that the race is not for the fastest. Because you worked longer and harder than another person, that does not mean that you will end up with more money than the other person.

So, in one parable, we see that someone did not exercise his faith at all because he spent his energy being judgmental and critical of his master. (Go to my website www.bookthatchangedmylife

for the whole story or parable. Also, please note that the Bible gave meanings for these parables. However, I chose to use these parables to find meanings that apply to the context of the message(s) of this book.) For this, and other reasons, that servant did not have the mindset and heart to take the risk of adding value to what was in his possession. Therefore, he ended up worse off than before he was given the opportunity to grow wealth.

In the other parable, we see that some individuals were willing to take a risk to attain something, but they did not prepare enough. Their inability or reluctance to see the abundance of resources that were available to them, and to use those resources, forced them to abandon their mission.

The final parable shows us that some people would set a goal for what they want to accomplish, and how much in returns, pay, or profit they want to make from that accomplishment, job, or event. These people become successful and get exactly what they negotiated or planned to work for. However, they placed a cap or settled for a fixed limit on their returns. So, when they get the amount that they have limited themselves to receive, and notice that others who did less work in less time get paid in a value that equates theirs, they become displeased and disgruntled. They call it unfair and start thinking the individual who seemed to put in less time and work is not deserving of their reward. This gets seriously funnier because if in this parable, the "late starters" got to keep their individual pennies, but the "early starters" were given an additional penny, the "early starters" would likely have stopped complaining about the penny that the "late starters" got.

So, it was really not the amount of money that the late starters received that was the problem for the early starters; it was the thinking and perspective of the early starters that made them dissatisfied, jealous, and disgruntled. They allowed the thinking of what others received to prevent them from finding value and success in what their faith in a day's work had brought them.

I am always working on increasing my faith, and it is clear how you too can increase yours: "faith *cometh* by hearing, and hearing by the word of God," Romans 10:17 (KJV)—not by comparing your life and your possessions in a destructive way to that of others.

The greatest faith that God wants us to have is faith in Jesus Christ and His power to help us live a Christ-like, Christian life. That includes wanting us to exhibit faith in all other areas of our lives like health, relationship, vocation, and time and money. He wants us to live confidently through, with, and by a faith that is rooted in Him, and to live so regardless.

It is interesting that Abraham believed in what God promised. Even though God promised a son to Abraham who would be a deliverer, Abraham looked at his physical body and said, "Look at me. There is nothing in me in my old age that has the vigor to produce this promised son." However, Abraham believed God's words and that God was able to do what he, Abraham, could not do. God promised him and, because of God's trustworthiness, Abraham had faith that the promise that was going to be, already was. God's word is the substance of our faith. It was not some extraordinary magic that existed within Abraham. It is application of faith, or living in absolute belief of God's word, that brings miracles to pass.

Your source, God, has the provision and knows the path to how you can access it, even when you see no way. In case you do not identify as a Christian, and you are thinking, "Well, Abraham was a Christian, and that is the only reason why God blessed him. I agree that God's people do have favour. I also am aware that many Christians lack faith to tap into such favour, and they struggle while abundance is right at their feet. On the other hand, I see some non-Christians faring well. The Bible says that God sends rain to fall upon the just and the unjust (Matthew 5: 45). This means that God's abundance of wealth in the universe is available to Christians and non-Christians alike. Whoever taps into this abundance with good intentions and actions, will be blessed. Apply faith as you apply lotion, because it reflects and displays your Source to the world as your wealth increases!

> Apply faith as you apply lotion, because it reflects and displays your Source to the world as your wealth increases!

When a Christian sets out to attain riches, there must be no failing. Your God or Source is constant; so, ask yourself, "Why has my faith dwindled today?" You will find that you are giving more thought to some external factor, stealing your progress and jeopardizing your knowing that God will provide a way out of that situation. Or, you may be leaning only on your own strength that leads only to you becoming overwhelmed and afraid of what the future holds for you. Faith is enduring and relational; it is not about self, so that you become a pendulum in the wind. If you truly believe in God as your source, then you cannot ever truly say that you lose faith in getting out of poverty. To claim the latter, and say that you believe in God's love and abundance simultaneously, is paradoxical. You are also calling God a liar because the Bible in Psalm 24 declares that the earth, with everything and everyone that is in it, is God's. As Walt Disney puts it, if you believe something, believe in it all the way! You must believe that God has the universe under his control and that the universe will meet you back with resources you need because you have already put out to the universe that you are actively expecting something. That is FAITH. It is not *if*, it is *when.*

The ups and downs of your life are a manifestation of highs and lows of your thoughts and imaginations that are from your perceived views of reality. Our prayers, hopes, and faith are realized maximally when they are harmonized with our thoughts and actions. Bring your thoughts and actions in line with your Source of Faith.

> Our prayers, hopes, and faith
> are realized maximally when
> they are harmonized with
> our thoughts and actions.

*"Now **Faith** is the confidence in what we hope for and assurance about what we do not see,"* Hebrews 11:1 (NIV). Faith is a way of life, and we are the masters of our faith based on where we choose to root our faith and what we choose to think upon. Faith also means living intentionally or on purpose. Living intentionally means you are choosing daily to practice living now the way you want to live—in line with your thoughts and vision of your future. The effective calling and application of your faith is significantly affected by the vision you have for your life. If you allow it, Chapter 4 will take you into a better vision for your life.

Valerie's Infinity Note: Wealthy Christians spend more of their time focusing on the possibilities of where their faith will take them, rather than on the restrictive and repetitive "what-if-I-fail," "I'm stuck," or "maybe God doesn't want me to wealthy" narrative, which poor Christians tend to live within. Wealthy Christians know the foundation of their faith, but they also know that *they are responsible for the quality and application of their faith.*

Activity Time: Download workbook (value $37) for free.
www.bookthatchangedmylife.com

Chapter 4

VISUALIZATION

"Where there is no vision, the people perish ..."
Proverbs 29: 18.

What is Visualization?

Before you read any further, pause here and think. What does visualization mean to you? What are some negative and some positive things that come to mind if you were to hear someone say they are engaging in visualization? Do you think that visualization belongs to a particular cultural, religious, or other group?

In simplest terms, visualization is the process of using your imagination to create your world. In Christian vernacular, it is *divine guidance.* It is the *sight* of faith.

Visualization is the SIGHT of faith;
the process of using your imagination
to create your world.

Is Visualization Scriptural?

Hebrews 11:3 (NLT) reads: "By faith, we understand that the entire universe was formed at God's command, that what we now see did not come from anything that can be seen." So, yes visualization is scriptural. God created this world from His vision—nothing physical.

God also created human beings in his own image. The Bible states, "So God created human beings in his own image. In the image of God he created them; male and female he created them," Genesis 1:27 (NLT). God created human beings from the image or the vision he had for us. By virtue of God being a visionary and creating us in his image, we too are visionaries by nature! I am a visionary; you are a visionary. What did you do as a child at every moment you got? If you think you forgot, think about what you observe any child doing. You observe them using their imagination and doing creative things like assembling objects, expressing representations of how they perceive things and people to look like through drawing, and telling stories. For a child, it is all about creativity and the visions in their mind. A child will take a toy airplane and create an imaginary, exciting trip around their imaginary world with it. This too is visualization (or daydreaming: dreaming up a story while awake). We do not have to force it; it is innately a part of us. For those of you who may have gotten out of touch with this part of you, you can practice your way to it again. If you feel afraid because you have a history of bad memories, now you get to create better things. Do not allow bad events and experiences to permanently take away this invaluable quality God has innately placed in you. Your ability to have visions and use your imagination is part of your greatest power.

Some adults do not use visualization to their benefit because their lives have become so very busy that almost every imagination you have is about fear of how your situation is or could get worse. If you spend time daily thinking about and mentally seeing how broke you may be in the future, and envisioning your situation as hopeless, you must immediately get a handle on that. Start the practice of noticing that you allow your thoughts and mind to linger on such things, and change it. You already read under the sub-topic of "Metacognition" that you must *notice what you are noticing*.

For a simple activity of how you can begin to change your vision to one that is more desirable and that you actually want, take a moment and visit www.bookthatchangedmylife.com. You literally can take one minute to get this piece of information that will have, if you apply it, a lifetime effect on your life, on the lives of others close to you, and quite possibly on generations to follow your line.

How can you accomplish something definite without clearly knowing what you wanted in the first place? You must have a vision of where you want to go or else life will take you wherever it wants. If you do not have a clear vision of what you want, you run the risk of getting things that look very close to what you wanted but are not exactly what you had set out to get. Worse yet, you might accept this similar thing that you got, become satisfied with it, and miss out on the ideal one. Wealthy people develop a vivid vision of what they want to accomplish, and they work relentlessly and wisely to get it. Poor people, on the other hand, normally make general statements, which reflect the quality of their vision. They would say, "I need *some* money" or "I want to lose some weight," and so on. A wealthy, or wealthy-minded person, would instead say, "I need $10,000" or "I need to lose 7lbs (pounds)." You are likely to achieve a goal that you envisioned in a definite way much easier than one that you are uncertain about. **Visualization is what gives the edge in clarity of your purpose in order to get desired results.**

Visualization is a fundamental part of the faith process. One cannot have effective faith without seeing and planning their goals and future. The latter part of Hebrews 11: 3 states: "... that what we now see did not come from anything that can be seen." Wow! That is powerful and true. How can one see something that does not appear? Put another way, how can one see something, or anything, that does not have a physical constitution? The answer lies with the mind; the answer lies with faith; the answer lies with purposefulness. You must guide your mind to believe in events that you want to be made manifest in your life. I use the work guide in recognition of your individual ability and choice to make things happen.

Purpose of Visualization

The purpose of visualization is to give clarity to the pursuits of your heart through faith. As your vision matures and becomes stronger and clearer, your passion, emotion, and energy are also very involved. This means that your reality is now first being created in your mind and, if you put in the necessary work, it will, in due course, be manifested through energy into the physical realm where others can observe and notice your creation. If you cannot see it, then you cannot get it!

The reason why some individuals struggle so much with accomplishing their goals is because they are superficial about it. They set goals but do not plan out and visualize it enough. You must anchor your vision with faith and emotion; live like it is real. If you want to build a lasting movement, you must engage with your vision and be one with it. Do not treat your vision like just another thing that you will try to make work. Unite with it. Your vision is a part of you. **When others see you, they should also see your vision emanating from your lifestyle.**

Words of Vision

Matthew 12: 36-37 says that every single person will have to give an account for every idle word that they speak, and *the words we say will either acquit us or condemn us.* This is extremely serious stuff. Words have power! In fact, words have creative power! I believe we were created to create, and our words are a tool assigned for this job.

First (1) Corinthians 2:13 tells us that words are not just noise; words are spirit. That is why when someone speaks words over your life, that person could be deceased for years, but their words still impact your life, if you let them. If the words were negative, and you have not learnt to rebuke what they have said against you by speaking life into your life and living above their remarks, you may still be reeling in doubt and vulnerability because of it. On the other hand, if your parents and teacher, or even a random stranger, spoke words of how productive you will be as an adult, some of you use that one positive moment to withstand much of the difficult events in your life. Their words remain a blessing in your life. This truth is based in Proverbs 12:18 (NIV), which says: "The words of the reckless pierce like swords, but the tongue of the wise brings healing." Verse 13 of first Corinthians, chapter two, reveals that you can choose to use and apply words taught from the perspective of human understanding, or you can use and apply words from a spiritual and uplifting perspective.

Strive to be always mindful of the words that you speak over your life, your children's lives, and the lives of all other human beings. Proverbs 18:21 says that death and life are in the power of the tongue, and those who love to talk will reap the consequences.

Part of the early history of the Israelites is captured in the Bible. Numbers 14:2-3 (ESV) says,

"And all the people of Israel grumbled against Moses and Aaron. The whole congregation said to them, 'Would that we had died in the land of Egypt! Or would that we had died in this wilderness! Why is the LORD bringing us into this land, to fall by the sword? Our wives and our little ones will become a prey. Would it not be better for us to go back to Egypt?'"

Here is a brief, basic context of the Israelite's situation: The Israelites were in bondage under slavery in Egypt. God promised to deliver them and told them that He would give them the land of Canaan, which is referred to as "the Promised Land" in the Bible. God literally parted a sea and let them walk through to the other side, away from their bondage and closer to the Promised Land. Now, please go back and read the preceding Bible text again. Notice that God kept his promise to them and got them away from Egypt out of slavery. As they walk away from slavery, God is actually leading them through Moses and Aaron, straight toward the land that he promised them. You would think that the Israelites would be very happy about this. However, the Israelites were stuck in their limited mentality and instead of keeping their vision on the land they were travelling to, they continually looked back or assumed the worst for their future. Although they did not yet arrive in the Promised Land, they allowed their fear to get the best of them. They focused their contagious, negative energy on a vision of what the people who inhabited the land would do to them when they arrived. They envisioned that the people would kill them—along with their wives and children. They cast away God's promise, His vision that He gave them, and fought against the direction for their lives after all of what God had brought them

41

through. Keeping their vision of the Promised Land, which God had already put in their hearts, and showing gratitude and confidence as if God had already delivered them from slavery, could have helped them get over the transient stumbling blocks on their journey. Keeping their minds on the vision would have helped maintain their faith and belief that God would *again* do what he promised. On the contrary, they complained, grumbled, and griped—they talked incessantly about how they were ready to give up on their goal of reaching the Promised Land. They went as far as to say that it might have been better if God had left them to die in Egypt.

You might be thinking, "How ungrateful?!" At the same time, this situation happens more often in our lives than we might acknowledge. When we grumble, complain, and focus on the past, the past situation is no longer the problem in our lives; we are now the problem because we are choosing to live in the past. Can you think of a time when you experienced a devastating event in your personal life? … Then, God got you out of the situation or showed you a way out? What did you do with that opportunity? Did you remain in your old condition by not using the opportunity at all, or did you get out of it but still allowed your mind and your conversation to dwell so much in the past situation that you were living as if you were still stuck in it and had not made any further progress with your life?

I encourage you to refrain from grumbling and moaning about a situation or person while there is still hope. When God gives you even a glimpse of your vision of your way out of an undesirable situation, immediately go toward that light or path. If you move as much as possible in that direction, and keep your humble mind on God, He would progressively open doors every step along the way until you exit that situation.

If you want to reach *your* Promised Land, you must walk *your* journey. The bumps are not meant to cause you to abandon your mission. All of the bumps you experience along the way, and get over, are actually building your character for what you are about to receive on arrival.

If you come across a Bible, please read James 3: 5. It talks about how the tongue is a small part of the body but how boastful it can be. It continues to say that just like a small flame can cause a great forest fire, so can the tongue defile the entire body if not used wisely. Human beings have been able to control and tame every species of beasts and animals, but humans find it difficult to tame the tongue. The tongue can be used for curses or to suppress lives but, thank goodness, it can be used for praise, to cancel curses, and to build and uplift ourselves and each other. Positive words can greatly improve our situations and relationships in our homes, as well as in our business and social lives.

Transformation (Transformed by Vision)

Vision creates passion and energy in us and others. It is the moving force in life. Visualization allows you to fulfill your destiny in nature. All things are created twice—first in the mind, then in nature where it is visible to our naked eyes. Second (2) Corinthians 4: 4 talks about how the **minds** of some people were **blinded**, and these people continued living in their old ways as if they were incapable of change. Just like your eyes allow you to experience physical vision, your mind is always readily available to produce your vision or insight.

In a type of therapy called Individual Psychology, or Adlerian Therapy, named after Dr. Alfred Adler, one of the stages of change that we, as therapists, help clients through is called Insight. During the Insight stage, we help clients find the meanings and values that they associate with their dysfunctional way of living. You might wonder why we would want clients to find value in their dysfunctional way of living. Here is the answer: It is not that we are helping them create value in such a non-productive and inhibitive way of living, but we are helping them process their life experience to help them become aware of the unhealthy internal and external patterns they engage in daily. If clients continue to see benefits in their dysfunctional way of living, it remains difficult for them to change for the better. They must learn to associate or get these benefits from healthier means. We then use our clinical skills and understanding of the process of self-actualization to help our clients look internally and become aware of how their current way of living is restricting their opportunities in life. It is until clients come to terms with this that we mutually agree to begin more focused work toward another stage called Reorientation. Reorientation includes clients' conscientious decisions to move away from their old ways of thinking and behaving, and toward more effective, courageous, and functional ways of living. Insight comes before Reorientation, simply because it would be next to impossible for you to make meaningful and lasting change without identifying and acknowledging what in your current life is not serving your vision or greater good. It would make your life so much easier as you take on new challenges of growth.

The problem with many people today is that they want to change on the outside so that they can show off to the world but, in hastily doing so, they overlook the fundamental work that needs to be done on their insides. As a result, their wealth and relationships do not stand the tests that come because their foundations were not built solidly. True transformation must be built on a strong *inner* foundation—yours, not someone else's. Romans 15: 20 (NIV) says, "It has always been my ambition to preach the gospel where Christ was not known, so that I would not be building on someone else's foundation."

You must protect your minds like you protect your eyes. You do not leave your eyes carelessly exposed to the elements. In fact, we have built-in reflex responses to protect our eyes. If the sun is too hot, we squint; if a fly or dirt particle moves by our eyes, we adjust our eyes, shift our heads, or automatically use our hands. If you notice an unusual tiny growth in your eyes or unusual mucus coming from your eyes, you take immediate cautionary actions, all for the sake of protecting your eyes.

Now, let me ask you, do you protect your mind this way? Your mind is your inner eye. Are you on guard for what attempts to enter, form inside, or leave your mind? Do you spend most of your waking moments living in the past and reminiscing on how you have been hurt? Or how much pain you are in? Or how you would like someone else to be hurt because of what they have done to you? Or how you can never move forward? Do you know that every moment you recreate and refresh the problem by using the power of your mind, you also mentally put yourself through that awful past event again? That is why your joy is not being restored.

As a psychotherapist, I strive to ask my clients as much as possible to step out of their immediate physical environment that they believe is causing them undue stress. By allowing your physical eyes to focus on other people, cars, buildings, trees, communities, etc., you trigger other better sensations in your brain that subconsciously gives you a glimmer of hope. This activity lets you physically see that the physical world is bigger than your immediate physical, stressful environment. Likewise, if you reflect and find that your mind and words are heavy with unpleasant memories and a poor outlook on life, please do the following:

Discipline yourself for at least one minute a day to think about a positive situation that is significantly opposite of your negative thoughts. Get yourself totally engrossed in that positive experience. Take action, and do this for 7 days diligently, and experience your first step into your *new thought* life and *mindset.*

Every change that you wish to create for a better life must be followed by targeted action before you get results. Chapter 5 unleashes how a life of disciplined actions must manifest its vision in due season. This chapter will help you break through your real and perceived barriers into a more fulfilling life as it teaches the relationship between faith, belief, knowledge, vision, and action.

Valerie's Infinity Note: Wealthy Christians know that the ability to create a vision for their lives is one of human's greatest gifts, so they use that gift to work for them. They understand that *God used vision to create the universe and, since they **are created in His image**, that they also have the gift of vision, with or without physical sight,* to design their lives the way they desire it to be. They know that since the beginning, ***everything is created twice****:* firstly, in the spiritual realm, or mind, and, secondly, into the physical world and to our naked eyes.

Activity Time: Download workbook (value $37) for free.
www.bookthatchangedmylife.com

Chapter 5

TAKING ACTION

Action is the process of doing something, normally with the hope of resolving a situation or getting something done.

Action Is The Breath Of Faith

If you are not taking action, but you say you have faith, you are deceiving yourself. Faith, without action, is dead. So, for all you Christians out there who say you have faith that God will bless you with wealth, but you are just sitting around and waiting for him to drop everything in your lap, I have wake-up news for you—it likely *ain't gonna happen!* If you find yourself in a complacent condition where you feel stuck in asking yourself "what if …?" and have been idling around for a while, it means that you are most likely engaged in your own head, refusing to make a decision because of fear. Action is not separate from faith. Action is the breath of faith. Faith in *action* reveals more Faith! … and this is your ticket to wealth.

> Action is the breath of faith.

To a Christian, taking action toward becoming financially free or attaining wealth means that you are applying and working your Faith. The Bible in James 2:20 (NIV) asks: "O foolish man, do you want evidence that faith without deeds is worthless?" This text is for the individuals who do not want to take action on what *they* call faith. They do not know or do not want to believe that they have no faith at all. The text says that it (their faith) is dead; but they think that what they believe is faith and want someone else who challenges them on that to provide evidence that their faith is dead. Such a person is called a foolish man or woman. They are foolish because all an individual needs to do is take a look at himself or herself and the manifestations in their life to see that what they called faith has yielded no results. They do not need someone else to prove their faith for them. In fact, no one else can prove your faith for you. Only your actions and results can reveal your faith to you.

If you think you have faith, but you are not taking action, what you have is belief, not faith. But belief alone cannot transform you into your best self. The Bible says, in James 2:19 (NLV), that "You say you have faith, for you believe that there is one God." Good for you! Even the demons believe this, and they tremble in terror." This text speaks for itself. Even demons know that God is God, and believe it, and get scared as a result. Yet they do not honour God. This situation reveals that knowledge alone is not faith. Some of you have so much knowledge that you can teach a football stadium different information, one person at a time, and still have new information left to share. Yet you are broke and struggling. Faith is bigger than belief. Belief is bigger than knowledge alone. Belief and knowledge can strengthen your faith. Faith is bigger than action alone, but faith is naught without action. Faith is more belief of knowledge in *action!* Put another way, **faith** is more of using your **belief** in some **knowledge** that you have to **act** in line with your **vision**.

Faith is knowledge, belief, and decision in action that is in line with your vision!
Faith is about relationship!

Taking Action

To get out of poverty means wisely working your way out of poverty. If you are not living in poverty but you want to become more financially independent, or you are rich but want to become wealthy, the same rule applies—you must work strategically toward that goal. To put it another way, you must DO your way out of poverty. The Bible, in Proverbs 10:4 (NLV), says lazy people are soon poor; hard workers get rich. Now, the Bible said it—I didn't! Since the Bible only tells truth, if you do not agree with this statement, it must mean a few things, including:

i.   You are a diligent, hardworking person, but you are not working efficiently.

ii. You may be trading your time for money instead of trading the value of what you have and do for money.

iii. You may be in a work, personal, or social relationship, where someone, or an organization, is exploiting the rewards of your labour so you do not get to enjoy them yourself.

iv. You may be lacking knowledge or resources on how to invest the little possessions you already have to make more wealth for you.

v. You may be taking in large sums of money but you lack self-control in your giving and spending.

vi. You may be truly working hard but in doing a job or running a business that you do not like, and that makes your performance feel like it is tougher than it actually is; as a result, you genuinely feel like and think that you are working harder.

A dream supported with daily, consistent, and relevant action must move closer to its realization. You will never eventually lose by taking informed targeted actions toward your goal. You can only win by taking action. If you take an action and that action does not work out, you are left with wisdom and narrowed direction that puts you in a better position to attain that desired goal.

"Just as the body is dead without breath, so also faith is dead without good works," (James 2: 26; ESV).

When some Christians think about Spirit, they tend to think about people speaking in tongues or dancing all over the church floor. However, not only tongue-speaking and dancing Christians share the Spirit of God. Every single person has some of God's Spirit in them. When God created man and woman, he breathed into their nostrils the breath of life, and man and woman became living souls. This is found in Genesis 2: 7 in any Bible. The Spirit also covers the breath of life, which every living human has. This is understandable since life is only of God. Therefore, everyone shares in the gift of God's spirit. That is why every human has the potential for salvation. Whether or not people acknowledge it, and honour God to represent that, is a different matter. Some people decide to use this holy gift of life called breath or breathing to do wrong, and their behaviours overshadow the true intent for their lives.

The text says that without breath, your body is dead. We all know that. The text also says that without good actions, our faith is dead. Why do we not acknowledge that? Is it because we are lazy? After all, we do not have to deliberately take each breath (unless one is in poor health) so we claim that part of the text; on the other hand, we do have to intentionally produce good work for our faith. So, instead of acknowledging that our faith is dead and that we are responsible for that, we complain and blame other people, things, and God to keep our false pride and escape the responsibility for a better life.

Again, James 2:26 (NIV) reads: "As the body without the spirit is dead, so faith without deeds [or action] is dead." If the Bible analogizes the body with faith, and action with spirit, it literally means that your faith has no value until you take action. If you say you have faith, but your faith does not have works, your kind of faith will not save you from sin, from ill health, nor from poverty (James 2:14). All change demands action. It makes sense that this is so, because if by some mental processing alone you could fully create change, the world would be a very chaotic place. Slothful and unwise people would bring about all types of things that they are not mature enough to follow through on. What a mess that would be to clean up.

When we step out from fear and step into applying ourselves to attain our goals, our lives remain more stable when we get our results. Why? Because living by the principle of faith in action changes us in the process. And is not this—personal growth and changes to become your best self—the greatest thing that can happen? Yes! So, go afraid; go trembling—but Go out into action!

Christians love to talk about the faith of the person called Abraham in the Bible, but very rarely do they talk about the courageous actions that he took. Without his actions, there would be one less amazing Bible story of faith to talk about and maybe no legacy to remember Abraham by. Abraham was a man of action because he knew his actions, and only his actions, would truly reveal to the world and confirm to himself that he is a man of faith in God.

Types of Actions

I. The Hustle

Make every minute count. Get out of playing with your ideas in a perpetual mental way and get into gear by taking action. Some of you talk so much about your faith in an idea that someone else listens to you, takes your amazing idea, gets into action, and makes a business or money on your intuition or idea; and all while you are still talking about what a good idea you have. You must learn to take quick action and redeem every "free" time you have.

II. The Yearn

Yearning or desire is that strong feeling that is mixed with a spiritual connection to something you really want or want to see happen. It is yearning that helps us withstand the challenges as we take action toward achieving a goal. Basically, you have faith that your desire will be manifested from taking this action.

Everybody get to experience a desire for a better life. The majority of people choose not to act on that desire. When you stifle your hearts desire, your passion to pursue it suffocates and dissipates. This lack of, or fight against taking, action kills your potential to be all you can be and zaps your zest for life. If you continue to resist yearning actions on things the heart, you may wake up one day and wonder where your life went, or that you did not live a life of courage and quality.

You sometimes have desires in your lives, but you are still not taking action. This means that you are probably waiting for your back to be up against a wall for you to take action. While this is still a start, you must put your desire into a vivid vision and develop the habit of taking actions to accomplish goals because you, as a person, will become a better person in the process. You must know your "WHY" and you must come up with some daily habits to help establish your state of taking actions to succeed. You must take action to any goal and work at it in order to come into your full potential. If you create a pattern of taking even small actions, and you start getting good results, that will motivate you to continue the practice. If you don't stop, and your actions get more deliberate, specific, and bigger, you can bet that you are moving toward success; in fact, you can happily say that you are succeeding.

III. Rapid-Massive Action
Rapid-Massive Action means acting on something you know that you must do *immediately* and *in the biggest way* you possibly can. Rapid action leads to rapid progress. It comes with big risks but, at the same time, can lead to huge success.

IV. "Just Because" Action
This is where you take action because you want to be part of a circle where everyone else is doing something. Such action does not come from a personal or soulful place of desire. Instead, it is likely coming from a place of fear, scarcity, and covetousness. This is the opposite of taking action based in desire. This type of action is often short-lived; however, you can learn from it that you have what it takes to work on your goals. All you need to do is create your own vision and tailor your actions accordingly.

V. *Tentative Action*

Tentative action is the type of action you take when you say, for example, "I would really like to own my home or transition from my nine-to-five job to investing fully in my business, or write a book, but I'm giving it three months. Then, if it doesn't work, I'll just do something else."

While it is sometimes valuable to put timelines on our objectives and goals, you must first assess what that goal means to you. If you do not do that, you will find yourself in a dangerous pattern of starting projects and never seeing them to completion. My mom had an expression for that: "hot love ... soon cold." Individuals that get caught up in the habit of taking only tentative actions, tend to lack the discipline and perseverance necessary to build wealth and/or a fulfilling life.

VI. *Purposeful Action*

Unlike Tentative Action, Purposeful Action is exactly what its name suggests it is. It means: you have a vision or goal in mind; you believe you can accomplish it; its accomplishment depends on your decision to act or pursue it, and you have moved into doing something that will eventually get it done. Wealthy-minded people operate within this type of action also.

You are able to apply definitive attention and focus on taking purposeful action toward a goal because that goal is yours—you can see it, so you can reach it, because you own it in your vision from within. You take intentional action and actively, but patiently, wait for it to happen.

A baby takes nine months in their mother's womb before getting born into this world. I would hope that people can be as patient with their dreams for at least that long. Refrain from seeing it as a race, but see each action step you make as building goals of legacies that will last. Know that well because, when you start a business, for example, it does not mean that you have given viable birth to it as yet. Like in the case of a human, there is the mental planning, followed by the incubation period, then foundational developmental stages. This is where both you and the world can increasingly tell that you are pregnant with a child, but that child is still developing internally and not ready for the elements of this world. Then, when you give birth, it is nine months later, and that baby still needs nurturing but is ready for gradual exposure to the elements of living. So, be patient with your dreams and the progressive manifestation of their growth and the returns they will yield.

VII. Determined Action

Determined Action is almost identical to Purposeful Action except that the action that you take started solely as the result of a goal or vision laid on your heart due to an observed need of others. In other words, the needs of others determined your action. The vision is still yours; you are committed to this goal. That goal is coming from a place of need for you to serve others. As a result, you know that abandoning this goal is not an option, so you prepare yourself to ride out the waves and storms to see this goal come to pass.

Determined actions can be small or massive but, since you know in your heart that you are called to do it and others are depending on you, you take the leap into action despite the possible calculated consequences. You also stick to the process because you can already "taste" the benefits and see the potential change in others' lives when this goal is accomplished. Wealthy-minded individuals operate within this type of action taking also.

Acting, or acting in faith, requires sacrifice, shedding of things and people, some aloneness, and many tests, so that you are built strong and prepared to take care of what you are about to manifest/birth.

Willingness To Act Through Fear And Uncertainty Versus Dependency

Go scared. Go trembling. Go shaking. Go in faith. You must Go!

When we are uncertain, we feel vulnerable. This is a normal feeling, but it can lead us to search for any answer that will make us feel more certain and less vulnerable. However, searching for random answers to steer you into certainty can get you caught up in finding things that make you even more uncertain. Many of you might be able to recall a time when you wanted to do something and, because you felt some fear, you reached out for the opinions of others. The result of that was, because your friends are normally on the same level that you are, they did know how to help you move forward into that goal. Instead of motivating you and helping you explore positive possibilities, they told you how scared they would have been if it were them and pointed out all of the money and other support that you did not have to get the goal accomplished. After some time had gone by, you reflected on the situation and realized that your dependence on other people's opinions for moving forward with your goal actually demotivated you and contributed to your not accomplishing it. The majority of us have had that experience, and the result for us was usually spending months, and even years, stuck in the same place where we were trying to move out of in the first place.

To prevent this from happening, you must instead look at the WHY of your goal, which includes the value it will bring when you accomplish it. Also, focus on as many resources and as much support as possible that can get you to this goal; then, take a leap toward it. Ecclesiastes 11: 6 (NLT) says, "Plant your seed in the morning and keep busy all afternoon, for you don't know if profit will come from one activity or another—or maybe both." The universe rewards momentum, so you will find that as you take your first step toward achieving that goal, more doors will open up in the direction that is right for you.

In this chapter, you learned that disciplined, consistent, and informed actions are always rewarded. The next chapter will focus on a type of action that you must come to embrace and engage in if you want to grow in wealth.

Valerie's Infinity Note: Wealthy Christians take action on their faith and are not confused about the fact that *without action, faith is as dead—like a body without breath.* We are not waiting for God to just drop things on our laps; we work strategically toward accomplishing our vision and see God open doors as we move forward. We *do not confuse busyness with effective action or work*; neither do we work just so others can see us working; instead, we work tenaciously with eagles' eyes to achieve specific goals within our larger vision.

Activity Time: Download workbook (value $37) for free.
www.bookthatchangedmylife.com

Chapter 6

GIVING BACK

"Remember this: whoever sows sparingly will also reap sparingly, and whoever sows generously will also reap generously,"
2 Corinthians 9:6 (NIV).

The Principle Or Mission Of Giving Back

Giving back is a mission or principle because it did not start with us but was present from the beginning of time. Giving must go on and will go on with or without you or me. Think about it: the dynamics of the world is ever-changing, and its change is based on how anything and everything is shared—giving and receiving.

If you sow criticism, you will reap criticism; if you sow love, you will reap love; if you sow in kindness, you reap kindness. This is the principle established in the preceding text of 2 Corinthians 9:6. In fact, it is referred to as the Law of Sowing and Reaping, or the Law of Giving and Receiving. Another thing to let sink into your mind is that you always reap more than you sow; for example, if you sow a single kernel of corn, you generally will reap at least an ear of corn containing many kernels.

For those of you who have some discomfort with the preceding paragraph because you might have had an experience where you felt that you did not reap what you sowed, there is not much I can say to you other than to be actively patient—your time will come. However, the Laws of the Universe cannot be changed, as God is unchangeable. "God is not human, that he should lie, not a human being, that he should change his mind. Does he speak and then not act? Does he promise and not fulfill?" Numbers 23:19 (NIV).

Now, back to giving. In the Bible, one story is told of The Rich Young Ruler who met Jesus and asked Jesus about what he must do to be saved. He confidently and proudly told Jesus that he had kept all the commandments since he was a boy. Then Jesus asked him to sell all that he had and give the proceeds to the poor. The young man could not find it in his heart to do that and walked away from Jesus. He kept his wealth to himself and declined to follow Jesus and get more quality riches at a later date. The message in this story is that we must hold on to whatever we have, *but* loosely, because we never know when God will ask you to give up, transfer, or share what you have. Remember, we are stewards. If you knowingly love your "stuff" more than you love God, and are not doing anything to flip that around, then you are prostituting your soul. The Bible says, "Where your treasure is, there will your heart also be," (Matthew 6:21). That is why you have to honour God and be grateful for humble beginnings. If you do not have a bigger purpose for attaining wealth than just to "big-up" yourself, and if you are not grateful to God when you have only ten dollars, it will be very difficult to share, express gratitude, and honour God when you accumulate wealth. Your whole attention will be on getting more, and more, and more, in an attempt to fill that insatiable greed inside of you, but, as we all know, a greedy person can never be satisfied—well, maybe only temporarily.

Giving back reflects our gratitude for what we have.

The Quality Of Your Giving

When people say they are of God and love Him, but they are not givers, there is a major missing link in their relationship and knowing of who God is. How can you come to the awareness that you are a stingy individual, and say that you love and truly know God, and yet refuse to act Godly? God is a giver. If God is a giver, then we must be givers too. We are imitators of those we follow. If you keep holding on to everything you have, then you are not making room for other things that God and life has for you. Your withholding mainly signifies two things: you are stingy by choice, or you are struggling with your poverty mindset. In both situations, you are stagnating your inner growth in the wealth journey. The best thing that can come out of your accumulating wealth is that you become a better human being in the process.

I must add that when I encourage people not to be stingy, I do not mean giving away all that you have carelessly. Remember, you are a steward. In your management of what God has blessed you with, you must find a portion to bless others with.

When you are a stingy person, or give grudgingly, people may receive your gifts out of dire need or refuse it in spite of their need. In the Book of Genesis, in the Bible, a man named Abraham (whom I referred to earlier in this book) refused to accept some wealth from an enemy because Abraham did not want his enemy to say that it was the enemy who made him rich.

Both giving and receiving should be done out of love. When we help others grudgingly and out of obligation, or when we force people into giving us things, we block the experiential blessing that builds our human spirit in the process. "Each of you should give what you have decided in your heart to give, not reluctantly or under compulsion, for God loves a cheerful giver," 2 Corinthians 9:7 (NIV). There are times when receivers must be strong and remain waiting on the lord to bless them from his selected source, and not just receive things from anyone.

Some Benefits of Giving:

- Giving expresses faith and shifts your thinking away from a consciousness of scarcity to one of abundance.

- Giving attracts favour. People who share a lot often have favour in their lives.

  - Favour is something that money cannot buy but, when you give, God in turn puts an attraction on your life that brings people your way to use their power, abilities, influence, and resources to help you.

- Giving obliterates fear and transforms your spirit into one of gratitude and love.

(If you would like my unabridged list of the benefits of giving, go to www.bookthatchangedmylife.com.)

The Not-So-Hidden Lessons In Returning Tithes

Tithes: Out of your 100%, return to God 10%, and watch God bless you with only 90%.

This relationship that God wants us to have with him that involves our money is fundamental to our relationship with others. It teaches us principles for our inter-human relationships. The principle of tithing teaches us that: we do not always have to fully understand a person's needs or reasons for asking for support before we give to that person; the basic amount of our giving does not depend on how much we make or have because it is the same relative amount for everyone—one tenth part out of the entire thing that you earned. If you earned ten cents, and you find it difficult to give a penny away, there is a very low probability that you will give away ten dollars out of your earned one hundred dollars, or one hundred out of your thousand, or one thousand out of your ten thousand. And imagine giving one hundred thousand dollars religiously out of each million dollars you earn!

I hope you see where I am going with this. Tithing is about something bigger and that money cannot buy. Tithing is a principle. When you develop the habit of tithing, regardless of your situation, you are practicing living your life by principles. If you lose, or never had, one million dollars out of which to give one hundred thousand, you should give ten dollars out of the one hundred dollars that you have, or a dime out of the one dollar that you have.

Such action shows God that you appreciate what you currently have, however little. If you do not have any money, then give off your smile or handy labour and favours to others. There is never a time when we cannot give. When we give off the little we think we have, we are doing ourselves a favour. We are keeping ourselves aware of what we truly have at the time. This awareness can help you see, and decide to change, some things in your personal life that are temporary barriers and hindrances to getting more.

Also, when you do not have money or other material possessions to give to people, but you choose to give off your kindness, volunteer at a community center, food bank, or nursing home, or iron someone's clothes, or cut a senior's grass, you are actually creating paths to wealth. God will cause what you have to multiply. He may cause someone with wealth to hear about your kindness and great attitude, and cause them to reward you directly for some of what you have done when you were not even looking for a reward or trying create a new opportunity for yourself.

Your obedience, trust, and faith in God are also tested when you tithe. God said that he will pour out abundant blessings on you when you follow the principle of tithing. Each time you choose not to tithe, you are showing God that you chose not to rely on his promise and, instead, steal from what he has given you. Look at the following Bible text from Malachi 3: 7-11 (NIV):

"Ever since the time of your ancestors, you have turned away from my decrees and have not kept them. Return to me, and I will return to you," says the LORD Almighty. But you ask, "How are we to return?"

"Will a mere mortal rob God? Yet you rob me." But you ask, "How are we robbing you?" "In tithes and offerings.

You are under a curse—your whole nation—because you are robbing me.

Bring the whole tithe into the storehouse, that there may be food in my house. Test me in this," says the LORD Almighty, "and see if I will not throw open the floodgates of heaven and pour out so much blessing that there will not be room enough to store it.

I will prevent pests from devouring your crops, and the vines in your fields will not drop their fruit before it is ripe," says the LORD Almighty.

"Then all nations will call you blessed ..."

The covert story of practicing tithing is that tithing benefits you, not God. God does not need you to return to Him what is already

His. He has the legal authority to claim it back anytime without notice. He is kind enough to share his resources with us and still *ask* us to share a small portion back to him, for which he, on top of that, promises to bless us. This is the best deal I have ever heard of: "I put all my wealth that I think you can manage in your hands. I tell you to use it responsibly and however you want until you die but with one condition—just give me one out of every ten things you generate from my wealth; you can keep nine out of the ten. And, oh, by the way, if you give me that one thing out of ten that I gave you, I will pour out more abundant blessings on you for your obedience to me." Anyone should want to accept this arrangement.

Another part of this covert story is that, technically, the small ten percent that we give back in obedience to God, goes to help our fellow human beings. So, God is not trying take from us, He is growing us and ensuring that we look out for each other and making life on earth better for everyone, especially you. He says that if you do as he says, he *promises* to prevent any and all outside forces from derailing your plans and vision, and make all of your hard work come to full fruition so that you will reap the rewards. What a good God!

Tithing in obedience to God can break generational curses. Go back to Chapter 2, if necessary, and refresh your understanding on generational curses. If your ancestors cheated God out of giving back, and passed on a lifestyle of greed, poverty, or selfish accumulation of wealth to you, the preceding text is saying that you can return to God to heal your family line from this sickness of greed, poverty, or selfishly accumulated wealth, by paying tithes.

You may not have understood the value of this principle before but, as your knowledge and understanding increases, you have a responsibility to yourself and to others to act in accordance with your gained wisdom. The amazing Maya Angelou once said, "I did then what I knew how to do. Now that I know better, I do better." Each piece of learning you receive on any of God's principles is an opportunity for you to get closer to Him. You can no longer choose to not practice a principle while fully well knowing that you are pretending to the world that you do not know it—what you are actually doing is lying to yourself and disobeying God. When you break a law, you must pay the consequence, as ignorance of the law is not an excuse for transgressing it. Imagine how sad it may be making God to know that you have what it takes to restore your life and the lives of your family line to Him, but you are choosing to live in your old ways as you feignedly ask God about why he is not allowing more blessings to come to you. Godly principles are as important as, if not more important than, some laws, because principles are preventative, restorative, and build character that keeps you from having to face laws and their consequences.

Given that tithing is a principle that is expected of us, it should be prioritized. It should be the first thing you do when you get your pay, harvest, or other form of reward. The quality of, including the attitude behind, our giving significantly determines the quality of our receiving. "Honour the LORD with your wealth, with the first fruits of all your crops; then your barns will be filled to overflowing, and your vats will brim over with new wine," Proverbs 3: 9-10 (NIV). If we make it our duty to give cheerfully in confidence with principle, God guarantees us an abundant life. God loves a cheerful giver, but even when we do not feel sure about giving, we should practice it. God did not ask us to feel good about it; He asked us to trust in his promise.

The Quantity Of Your Giving

When we talk about giving in relation to wealth, we tend to shift our mind to our spending currency. In doing so, we sometimes limit what we can give but also all that is available to us and that we can receive. Whatever you decide to give, this is the measurement by which it should be given. Second (2) Corinthians 9: 7 (NIV) gives us a guide, which says, "Each of you should give what you have decided in your heart to give, not reluctantly or under compulsion, for God loves a cheerful giver." You do not have to give anything you have if you do not want to. As stated above, it is good to practice it. However, you have an obligation to take time to decide on your giving or offerings to others. When you give from a cheerful sharing place, the person receiving your gift becomes blessed by your giving, and you also are blessed in the process. I have experienced this, and I'm sure you have too at some time in your life, where you have given something to someone, and your heart becomes so joyful in the process that it feels like you are the one who received the gift. Have you ever experienced that? We get this experience because not all gifts are tangible. In giving or sharing a tangible gift with someone else, we are receiving gifts in the form of happiness, fulfillment, and growth in our trust and faith, and favours back. It is a universal law, which is an automatic and natural process that occurs even when we fail to recognize it.

The verse continues to say that if you give from a place of cheerfulness, "God is able to bless you abundantly, so that in all things at all times, having all that you need, you will abound in every good work." This passage is saying that once you give from a place of contentment and abundance, you can count on it that everything will come back to you in one form or another. When you don't give, you are cheating yourself and cheating other people because wealth in any amount is meant to be shared.

When you read about the principle of giving and receiving, please do not understand it to mean that you must carelessly give away everything you have. For some of you, there are people in your lives who will use the goodness of giving to strip you of all that you have. Someone shared a Facebook post with me that read something like this: *people will take all of you if you let them. Give of yourself, but make sure you have some of you left for you.* Proverbs 21: 20 says: the wise person saves for the future, but the foolish man spends whatever he gets. Be diligent in your act of giving. This practice will translate to other areas of your life and build your habit of planning and discipline in ways that you never imagined.

As you come to the final chapter, you will have to decide how badly you want to succeed at your new prosperous vision for your life. You will have to discipline yourself into routine observation and pruning of your life. You will need to make decisions toward your future that will get people around you upset, but you will have to proceed the anyway.

Valerie's Infinity Note: Wealthy Christians know that if they give in abundance, they also reap in abundance. We give back to individual persons and communities using gifts &/or services. Personally, God has given so much to me that I am almost afraid and too humbled by his goodness and trustworthiness not to give back. Wealthy Christians give back, but they *give responsibly and with the understanding that they are only stewards of whatever they possess.*

Activity Time: Download workbook (value $37) for free.
www.bookthatchangedmylife.com

Chapter 7

PLANNING & DISCIPLINE FOR YOUR CHANGE

How Badly Do You Want It?

After you catch a vision of what it is you want to accomplish, you must work backward and put into a plan how you are going to realize that vision or achieve that goal. You cannot just sit back and hope that something is going to happen to you, and your goal will magically manifest before your eyes. Your goal is designed by you, and only you can direct your energy in a targeted way to accomplish that particular goal. Your planning must include the final goal, but all wealthy-minded people know that it is the discipline of the daily, weekly, and monthly objectives that must be attended to and completed in order to get to that eventual bigger goal.

God Planned

Even God planned. We are familiar with the creation Bible story: On Sunday, the first day of the week, God created light. On the second day, He divided the waters above from the waters below to call them heaven and earth, respectively. On the third day, God commanded the waters below to be in one place and called them sea. He called the dry place, land. On the fourth day, He created the sun, moon, and stars. On the fifth day, He created all the creatures that live in the waters and the birds that live in the air. On the sixth day, He created the creatures, which live on land. He also created man and woman but in his own image. Then, God took time and looked around and saw that what He had made was good. Then, on the seventh day, He made the day into a day of rest and called it The Sabbath Day, because it signified completion and Holiness.

God is the master planner, but all other successful and wealthy people plan and put their plan in as much details and specificity as possible. Here is a good place to start: Write down in as much detail as possible what you would like to accomplish. (Go to www.bookthatchangedmylife.com for further instructions on completing this important activity.)

Success Demands Planning and Discipline

The all-knowing God placed within us the ability to think, visualize, hope, plan, execute, and grow. If you planned something out and it didn't work, just consider that failure to be a part of the bigger plan, but keep moving forward.

I once heard the popular Brian Tracy say that, "Good habits are hard to form and easy to live with. Bad habits are easy to form and hard to live with." If you do not have clear plans for success in your life, you will unconsciously form new bad habits or struggle with old, unproductive habits that retard your growth and block your success. We are what we repeatedly do, so, to achieve excellence, we must practice new thoughts, and emotional and behavioural habits that are in line with our plan for success. In psychotherapy sessions, I often tell my clients that all habits are learned, even when it feels like you have had them all of your life. To "unlearn" undesirable habits, you *must* replace them with desirable ones. Once you plan and have written down your desirable habits, practice and repeat them until they become normal for you; thereby, gradually pushing the old habits into submission in your life.

To stick to your plan of forming new habits, you must apply self-discipline. Brian Tracy also said that "self-discipline is the ability to make yourself do what you should do, when you should do it, whether you feel like it or not." The Bible says that "No discipline seems pleasant at the time it is happening—it is painful! But afterwards there will be a peaceful harvest of right living for those who are trained in this way," Hebrews 12:11 (NLT). Another passage says, "A person without self-control or self-discipline is like a city broken down and left without walls," Proverbs 25:28 (ESV). If you do not practice self-discipline, you are leaving your dreams and visions open to be displaced by anything that passes your way; you are unprotected. Without self-discipline, you can kiss all of your plans for success goodbye. With self-discipline, your harvest will be great. You do not have to do this alone, even when it feels like you are alone; 2 Timothy 1:7 (NLT) reminds you of that. It declares that "…God has not given us the spirit of fear and timidity, but of power, love, and self-discipline." God has already placed what you need, to do this inside of you. So, get your plan into action and begin today. Your success begins the moment you start achieving small goals in your day to day living. Success and motivational speaker, Jim Rohn, said that success is something you attract by the person you become. As you discipline yourself and apply your plan, you are actually succeeding every step of the way. To walk in ranks of the rich and wealthy, you must be disciplined. Wealthy people do not have time for excuses as to why you could not keep an appointment or get your part of a task done in a partnership with them. Practicing self-discipline attracts successful people to you, and that is necessary to move you upward on your success path.

Relationships

The relationships you keep will, to a large degree, determine the quality of your journey to becoming your best self in all areas of your life, especially in wealth building.

Do not be too intimidated to associate with people who already have more wealth than you. Use their wealth status to fuel your inspiration that having more is possible for you, and as motivation to put in the hard work that will later pay off.

Sometimes keeping company with familiar people can keep you looking back and living in the past. Most times, they really do love you and are not even aware that they are holding you back. It is difficult for people who are close to you to see you in a different light. It is just the way that people generally operate. You must develop enough discipline and wisdom to love them but not depend on them to help you to the top. They do not understand your dream. It is futile thinking and unfair to expect people to fully understand your ambition when God did not give them your vision.

The sensitive part about relationships and success is when you have to sever ties with, or reduce the amount of contacts you have, with people you closely associated with. You may have to do that when they incessantly criticize your new behaviours toward your goal or try to remind you of your past faults and issues. You are not defined by your past; you are prepared by your past. Please, do not underestimate the power of negative or dead-weight people in your life. Proverbs 13: 20 warns us that whoever walks with the wise becomes wise, but the companion of fools will suffer harm. Similarly, 1 Corinthians 15: 33 warns us to not be deceived: "Bad company ruins good morals." Use your freedom to choose, build your new network of friends, and choose the amount and quality of time that you want to spend with family.

Note that even Jesus was not accepted in his own community. When a man named Nathanael heard that the savior was going to be from a place called Nazareth, Nathanael exclaimed, "Nazareth!

Can any good thing come out of Nazareth?" (John 1:46). Imagine how hopeless Nazareth and its people must have appeared, to have elicited such a remark from someone as smart as Nathanael. People might know that you live or come from a family of generational poverty, or from a violent and slum neighbourhood. What they do not know is the vision that God has put inside of you. You must be like Jesus: Do not totally ignore this attitude toward you as if it were not happening. Jesus accepted it for what it was. He did his best in his hometown and amongst relatives, but then he moved out of his hometown to accomplish his mission. His value was appreciated more in other places than in his own hometown.

Jesus got so much pushback in his own community that he said, "but I tell you the truth, no prophet is accepted in his own hometown," Luke 4:24 (NLT). I know you are not a prophet, and that is not the point. The point is that sometimes you have to forfeit the familiar and move into a place where people cannot hold your personal past, or the history that was left to you by others, against you, because they do not know your history. Not knowing your past will naturally cause your new environment to see you as you are now.

If you cannot move out of a suppressing environment at this time, immerse yourself with studying relevant scriptures and find free or paid online mentors. There is more than enough motivational and transformational content online to keep yourself in line with your vision until you are able to make your move.

Watch out for unpleasant energies from certain family members and relatives because, in the initial stages especially, you will have little time to mingle, and they may begin to think that you are choosing not to spend time with them. It is important to at least give family members a general idea that you are working on a project that will make you less available. When you do meet with your family, ensure that you spend quality, fun time with them.

Wealthy people spend most of their time with others who help to push them further into their purpose. Your immediate family, like children and your spouse, must always remain your priority, as long as the relationship is reasonably healthy.

Preparation And A Ready Mind

"For you know that when your faith is tested, your endurance has a chance to grow. So let it grow, for when your endurance is fully developed, you will be perfect and complete, needing nothing," James 1: 4-4 (NLT).

The blessing is already available. The earth already contains all of what you desire to have, in one form or another, for your better life. What you are working on is not so much the making of these things as much as the personal transformation of yourself into a person you must become to manage these things when you get them. When you have something valuable to manage that you have long been dreaming of, you have to make sure that you have been through the fiery process of shaping, reshaping, and disciplining that toughens you to appreciate and guard it with purpose.

Sometimes you will feel like you want to abort the process and journey of getting to your destiny because more difficulties keep coming your way. It is very possible that you probably are meant to learn a lesson and grow from those difficulties before you move further on. No lessons from your struggle will ever go wasted because each one will build your faith, strength, and perseverance and ability to manage bigger challenges that are ahead. Do not expect to obtain the medal without running the race. Far too many people chase after wealth and relationships, for example, without resolving it within themselves that they are willing to persevere through storms in order to achieve and manage them well. Sometimes you move from one situation to another situation, or one relationship to another relationship, only to find what you were running away from is present in the next one. If this is happening to you, do not just move again. Stop and see your situation for what it is—do not waste your living and experiences. Ask yourself why you somehow attracted the same situations and people over and over again. It is almost impossible to step fully away from it if you have not learnt from it. When you learn from this, you can then accept it for what it was and prepare yourself to be ready for your next level up.

Getting riches too easily, and before you prepare and ready your mind, can be your biggest headache.

One of my favorite virtual transformational millionaire speakers, and online mentor, Jim Rohn, left his amazing teachings behind. He often said that, "successful people do what unsuccessful people are not willing to do. Don't wish it was easier; wish you were better. Don't wish for less problems; wish for more skills. Don't wish for less challenge; wish for more wisdom."

Stop cowering under your journey's struggle; do not look at it as your identity of weakness. Call it your progressive struggle. Your struggles are your opportunities for breakthrough to victory but only if you face them. Your power and strength is revealed on the other side of your darkest pain: on the other side of your depression; on the other side of your anxiety and fear; on the other side of your bills; on the other side of your loneliness. On the other side of your victory is your realization that you have been made stronger with a ready mind. Your dark times are an invitation to get closer to God and to a better, victorious life.

Also remember that we serve a God who made a dry path in the middle of the sea, who makes a way in the wilderness, who rapidly calms a raging storm, who removed thousands of demons from a single man, who gives sight to people who are born blind, and who can go before you as your pillar of cloud by day to guide you, and your pillar of fire by night to give you warmth and light. God is ever present to be relied on in any of your life's circumstances; you must know that through your struggles. His strength is made perfect in our weaknesses. In other words, when you feel weak, despite giving all of your strength, you can tap into and rely on God's abundant strength.

Jesus taught his people that they could not *crown him* before they *cross him*. No cross; no crown. People generally want to talk about the victory of Jesus, but they do not want to spend time considering the cross he endured before he was crowned. The greatest legacies are the ones that are earned and built from your pain, discipline, sweat, and endurance. Matthew 26: 39 (NLT) reveals that even Jesus went through agony before he succeeded in his mission. The text reads, "He went a little farther and bowed with his face to the ground, praying, "My Father! If it is possible, let this cup of suffering be taken away from me. Yet I want your will to be done, not mine." Jesus was human; he too experienced the struggle on his journey to accomplishing his mission. He also knew that there was purpose in his pain, so he did not walk away from it; instead, he rested on God's power and strength to take him through. Imagine if Jesus did not come and die, and then resurrect; the world would see him as just one of us, and many would not follow him because he would have done nothing extraordinary and supernatural. It was His experience of being scorned and rejected, talked and lied about, physically and emotionally abused, and then murdered; but yet he resurrected, and that makes Him the significant person whom He lived on earth to be and who he lives to be in heaven. He went through all of this to lay the foundation for us to stand on.

People want to win the lotto and accumulate wealth, but they want to do it in a cheap way—they do not want to put in work. That is why some people lose their possessions just as quickly as they received them—they did not put in the work to build that foundation to withstand the elements that hit them.

"When the builders completed the foundation of the LORD's Temple, the priests put on their robes and took their places to blow their trumpets. And the Levites ... clashed their cymbals to praise the LORD ...," Ezra 3: 10 (NLT). Notice that they were not praising for the roof or the beautiful pews and windows. No, they were praising and were excited for the foundation because they knew that once a solid foundation was laid from hard labour, they would be grounded enough to better withstand all the expected or unexpected storms that would come their way. When your foundation is not built with security, you spend unnecessary time worrying because you know that you are living on shaky ground, or you ignore it and get tossed about by every wind, and then blame others and circumstances. The latter gets you discouraged, and discouragement ruins hope. Stay on a particular level and build your foundation; you will know when it is time to move. Do not rush wealth.

If you realize that you have done everything that you can on that level but only fear is holding you back from investing in your vision, then it is time to use your faith to move forward. Go slow if you have to, but make progress. The challenges of this past phase of your journey has prepared you for the next level. If you have been through terrible, difficult times, change your view of those experiences from how it beat you down. It was that way for a while, but you are still alive—there is still breath in you. You are tougher than ever before because you have been through all of those tests. You are now in a position to conquer obstacles, break down barriers, shatter ceilings and manage your critics. Be bold; go in and take what God has prepared for you. It will be difficult but not impossible. It is your time to decide to speak about your vision as if it already were. Do not speak of your future based on what it looked like from the past, or even what it looks like now, but speak of it only from the vision that God has placed in your heart.

Valerie's Infinity Note: Wealthy Christians are frequently planning. On an ongoing basis, you will find them encouraging themselves into expanding discipline necessary to follow through on their plans as they grow. They are not shy about receiving compliments and motivation from others either. Wealthy people plan for years ahead, then the individual years in between, then monthly, weekly, daily, and then down to the hours and minutes of a day. They work on being as efficient as possible with honouring their time. They know that if *God planned in order to execute his creation vision, we could not accomplish theirs without planning and discipline.*

Activity Time: Download workbook (value $37) for free.
www.bookthatchangedmylife.com

POINTS OF ENCOURAGEMENT

• In addition to improving the value of our individual and family lives, whatever you have stewardship over, or own, must also be used to include the greater good of others.

• Go ahead and be your best you. 3 John 1: 2 says that ABOVE ALL things, God wants you to PROSPER (wealth) and BE IN GOOD HEALTH (health) even AS YOUR SOUL PROSPERETH (spirituality).

• I know that we like to attribute the importance of faith, gratitude, action, and (mindfulness) visualization to significant motivational and transformational speakers, but all true laws of the universe or their concepts come from one Source— God. Evidence of that is found in the Bible. You can do the research yourself for confirmation.

• Use your ability to choose your thoughts, friends, movies, books, songs, and everything else wisely. Your life is the sum total of all of the little or big decisions that you make.

• We have many teachings on positive thinking, but positive thinking, while also fundamentally important, does not annul the words you speak over your life. Your words will build or break you because you speak out of the contents of your heart. Speak life!

- Pay attention to what you are allowing to flow freely around in your mind. If you do not direct what you keep your mind on and pay attention to, the unwanted stuff will eventually control you, even without you knowing it.

- Failure during building your desired lifestyle is never terminal, unless you make it so. Failure is a learning event that can help direct you to achieving your goal.

- Do not let life overwhelm you. Start where you are with what you have.

- Identify your *why*. Why do you see it as a must to change your life or change something about your life?

- Remember, the life that you live as a Christian may be the only thing some people will see as a reflection of God.

  - Are you living confidently in faith and reliance on God, even when your human mind does not see the best way out of your current unpleasant situation?

  - Are you doing all you can do with consistency and excellence?

- Are you practicing honesty and kindness, even when your situation makes it difficult to do so?

- There are times when life will get very tough, and your belief in yourself will be low. It is good practice to start surrounding yourself with people that believe in you and whom you can learn from.

- Distance the time, energy, and space you share with people who think you are out of your mind just because you have a dream for your life. Let me share one of my personal favorite beliefs with you: *People who are crazy enough to think they can change the world are the ones who do!*

- Do not expose yourself to others' negative responses to your building your dream life, and do not take their attitude personal. The dream is yours, not theirs. Only you will understand it and be committed to the experience of the journey. That is why only you will reap the greatest joy of the rewards.

- Begin your way out of poverty with prayers, and spending time reading your Bible. Then, practice your way out of the paucity of good thoughts by replacing old thoughts with uplifting ones that will do away with the habit of self-defeating thinking!

- As long as you have a dream in your heart for a better life, it is never too late to start working toward it.

- Do any meaningful thing that you can toward your better dream life, and do it every day!

- As mentioned earlier in the book, *apply faith like you apply lotion,* even when you do not know what the next step will be.

- The Holy Bible has all the resources of motivation and directions you need for your new life. Surrounding yourself with people who apply them and have results is a must for staying on your success path.

- You must DO your way out of poverty!

- Honour God as *You* **Take Action!**

Activity Time: Download workbook (value $37) for free.
www.bookthatchangedmylife.com

WELCOME TO CHANGE!

Now that you have read this book, do not go back to living life as usual. I wrote this book with the hope of igniting change in your life. Apply whatever touched your heart from this book to your life immediately.

All of the new or reinforced information that you have learnt should trigger new thoughts for change in your mind. Allow your new thoughts to lead to new choices. Your new choices should lead you to practice new behaviours. Your new behaviours will attract new experiences. Your new experiences should give rise to new emotions, which will automatically arouse new thoughts. And, as this process continues, you should move forward in the desired direction of your life. Always remember that *your life* is *your responsibility!* ... Honour it!

ABOUT THE AUTHOR

Valerie McIntosh is a graduate of Andrews University in the USA and York University in Canada. She currently resides in Canada with her lovely daughter. She is a registered psychotherapist and runs a private office in Toronto, Ontario, where she is well recognized for the work she is doing with youth and families. She also currently works with Canada's largest mental health agency. Here, she helps youth, who have experienced a first episode of psychosis, on their recovery journeys to transition into living an optimal, meaningful life. She served on the Adverse Events Reporting Committee and the Black History Committee, to name a few. She also served on the Board of Directors of the Ontario Society of Adlerian Psychology. Valerie is also a certified life coach, a role she uses to help others manifest positive results in relationships, vocation, health, time, and money. As a life coach, Valerie helps her clients transform their minds, abilities, and resources to achieve far beyond what many of them thought they ever could. She is an amazing transformational speaker. If you are looking for a coach or therapist to effectively transform the life of youth, Valerie is the person to depend on for results. As a compassionate, caring, and trusting professional, Valerie over-delivers quality by bringing so much success to others in "thinking-up," designing, and manifesting a life that is in harmony with your soul's purpose.

Valerie's background in Kinesiology and career development, combined with her experience as a Psychotherapist and Life Coach, puts her in an incomparable, unique position to understand and fulfill her clients' needs in a comprehensive way.

Valerie can be reached at valerie@bookthatchangedmylife.com.

Write Your Thoughts/Ideas Here:

The Book That Changed My Life

_____
_____
_____
_____
_____
_____
_____
_____
_____
_____
_____
_____
_____
_____
_____
_____
_____
_____
_____
_____
_____
_____
_____
_____

Valerie McIntosh